LifeLines

Life*Lines*

365 LIFE-ENHANCING
MEDITATIONS AND
INSPIRATIONS

GENERAL EDITOR: MARCUS BRAYBROOKE

DUNCAN BAIRD PUBLISHERS

LONDON

Life Lines
General Editor: Marcus Braybrooke

First published in the United Kingdom and Ireland in 2002 by
Duncan Baird Publishers Ltd
Sixth Floor, Castle House
75–76 Wells Street, London W1T 3QH

Conceived, created and designed by Duncan Baird Publishers

Editor: Louise Nixon
Editorial Consultant: Catherine Bradley
Designer: Rachel Cross
Picture research: Cee Weston-Baker

British Library Cataloguing-in-Publication Data:
A catalogue record for this book is available from the British Library

10 9 8 7 6 5 4 3 2 1

ISBN: 1-903296-54-4

Typeset in Trade Gothic
Colour reproduction by Scanhouse, Malaysia
Printed by Imago, Singapore

NOTES
Abbreviations used throughout this book:
CE Common Era (the equivalent of AD)
BCE Before the Common Era (the equivalent of BC)
b. born
d. died

contents

foreword

However storm-tossed our life's voyage might seem to us, there is always, in the depths of our inner being, a source of calm – if only we know how to find it. But amidst all the turbulence of our emotions and anxieties, and amidst the pressures of our worldly responsibilities, where do we even start to look?

Through the centuries many writers, astonishingly different in their personal circumstances and their beliefs, as well as in their social and historical settings, have succeeded somehow in putting into words profound thoughts that persuade us of certain universal truths and values. These ideas cut across distinctions of race, class, gender, age and religion. Some of the most inspiring of these writings are those that concentrate on peace, love and the spirit – for these are the things that really matter in life, whatever our faith and whatever our politics. These are the essentials that provide a foundation for living more at ease with ourselves, with each other, with whatever life brings us, and with the certainty of our mortality.

All the inspirations quoted in this book are reminders of the deep stillness and tranquillity we can find in a life of acceptance, simplicity, compassion, thankfulness, love and faith. In making contact with this stillness at the core of ourselves, we are touched by a power greater than our own. We can all draw strength, hope and renewal from this inexhaustible well of blessings.

If we detach ourselves from the distractions that oppress the spirit, all the energy previously absorbed in inner turmoil is set free to flow in love, for ourselves, our friends and our loved ones, all the people around us, all those who are suffering, even those who wish us harm – indeed the whole of humanity with whom we share a precious spiritual kinship.

Love and compassion can help us counter the conflict and violence within and between nations. Each of us can become a beacon of peace, radiating healing light into the world. Love for ourselves may seem at first rather self-centred, but self-love or self-respect is a vital foundation for love extended to others, and so sets the theme of the first section of this book, "The Centre of Being". From here the focus gradually spirals outward, through "The Inner Circle of Love" (covering such vital topics as compassion, karma, friendship, family) to "The Outer Circle of Spirit" – our relationship with the world at large and with the One within and beyond.

Read, reflect, and be inspired – if you find wisdom here, carry it with you, and enjoy its gifts to the full.

Marcus Braybrooke

The door to the human heart can be opened
only from the inside.

Spanish proverb

The centre of being

• True Self • Self-esteem • Inner Strength • Stillness
• Inner Wisdom • Giving • Thankfulness • Wonder • Being in Time
• Attentiveness • Nature • Acceptance • Simplicity • Happiness • Truth
• Wordlessness • Humility • Faith

true self

2 Me myself

Trippers and askers surround me,
People I meet, the effect upon me of my early life or the ward and
    city I live in, or the nation,
The latest dates, discoveries, inventions, societies, authors old
    and new ...
These come to me days and nights and go from me again,
But they are not the Me myself.

Walt Whitman (1819–92), from "Song of Myself", USA

3 Lute music

My soul gave me good counsel, teaching me that the lamp which I carry
does not belong to me, and the song that I sing was not generated from
within me. Even if I walk with light, I am not the light; and if I am
a taut-stringed lute, I am not the lute-player.

Jalil al-Din Rumi (1207–73), Persia

4   *Tea at the Palaz of Hoon*

Not less because in purple I descended
The western day through what you called
The loneliest air, not less was I myself.

What was the ointment sprinkled on my beard?
What were the hymns that buzzed beside my ears?
What was the sea whose tide swept through me there?

Out of my mind the golden ointment rained,
And my ears made the blowing hymns they heard.
I was myself the compass of that sea:

I was the world in which I walked, and what I saw
Or heard or felt came not but from myself;
And there I found myself more truly and more strange.

Wallace Stevens (1879–1955), USA

5 A free mind

A free mind is one which is untroubled and unfettered by anything, which has not bound its best part to any particular manner of being or worship and which does not seek its own interest in anything but is always immersed in God's most precious will ... . There is no work which men and women can perform, however small, which does not draw from this its power and strength.

Meister Eckhart (1260–1327), Germany

6 Self-knowledge

This is the miracle of life: that each person who heeds himself knows what no scientist can ever know: who he is.

Søren Kierkegaard (1813–55), Denmark

7 . *Within the circle of self*

Two exercises at life's beginning: to narrow the circle round about you more and more, and to check, again and again, that you are not hiding somewhere outside that circle.

Franz Kafka (1883–1924), Austria

8 *Mirror image*

The Self exists both inside
and outside the physical body,
just as an image exists inside
and outside the mirror.

From the Ashtavakra Gita *(c.200BCE–c.200CE), India*

self-esteem

9   *A drop in the ocean*

We ourselves feel that what we are doing is just a drop in the ocean. But if that drop was not in the ocean, I think the ocean would be less because of that missing drop.

Mother Theresa of Calcutta (1910–97), India

10   *The golden eternity*

Remember the golden eternity is yourself.

Jack Kerouac (1923–69), USA

11   *Compassion*

If your compassion does not include yourself, it is incomplete.

The Buddha (c.563–c.483BCE), India

Look within

12

If the eye were not sun-like, it could
not see the sun; if we did not carry
within us the very power of God, how
could anything God-like delight us?

Johann Wolfgang von Goethe (1749–1832), Germany

inner strength

13   *The breakthrough*

And the day came when the
risk to remain tight in a bud was
more painful than the risk it took
to blossom.

Anaïs Nin (1903–77), France

14 Destiny

If you will not fight your battle of life because in selfishness you are afraid of the battle, your resolution is in vain: nature will compel you.

From the Bhagavad Gita *(1st–2nd century), India*

15 The gift of fortitude

Nothing happens to any man which he is is not formed by nature to bear.

Marcus Aurelius (121–80), Roman emperor

16 Difficulties

It is not because things are difficult that we do not dare; it is because we do not dare that they are difficult.

Seneca (c.4BCE–c.65CE), Rome

17 Comrades in creation

I am no more lonely than a single mullein
or dandelion in a pasture, or a bean leaf,
or sorrel, or a horse-fly, or a humble-bee. I
am no more lonely than the Mill Brook, or a
weathercock, or the north star, or the south
wind, or an April shower, or a January thaw,
or the first spider in a new house.

Henry David Thoreau (1817–62), USA

18 Intimacy

I can be alone,
I know how to be alone.

There is a tacit understanding
between my pencils
and the trees outside;
between the rain
and my luminous hair.

The tea is boiling:
my golden zone,
my pure burning amber.

I can be alone,
I know how to be alone.
By tea-light
I write.

Nina Cassian (b.1924), Romania

19 Ride on singing

If you have a fearful thought, do not
share it with someone who is weak:
whisper it to your saddle-bow, and
ride on singing.

King Alfred of Wessex (c.849–c.901), England

20 The self-reliant soul

The poise of a plant, the bended tree recovering
itself from the strong wind, the vital resources of
every vegetable and animal, are also demonstrations
of the self-sufficing, and therefore self-relying soul.
All history from its highest to its trivial passages is
the various record of this power.

Ralph Waldo Emerson (1803–82), USA

21 Gentle strength

Good doors have no bolts
    yet cannot be forced.
Good knots have no rope
    but cannot be untied.

Lao Tzu (c.604–c.531BCE), from the Tao Te Ching, *China*

22 *The storm of fear*

The wise man in the storm prays to God, not for
safety from danger, but for deliverance from fear.
It is the storm within that endangers him, not the
storm without.

Ralph Waldo Emerson (1803–82), USA

23 *A favourable wind*

The wind of God's grace is incessantly blowing. Lazy
sailors on the sea of life do not take advantage of it.
But the active and the strong always keep the sails of
their minds unfurled to catch the favourable wind and
thus reach their destination very soon.

Mahatma Gandhi (1869–1948), India

The Plot Against the Giant

First Girl
When this yokel comes maundering,
Whetting his hacker,
I shall run before him,
Diffusing the civilest odors
Out of geraniums and unsmelled flowers.
It will check him.

Second Girl
I shall run before him,
Arching cloths besprinkled with colors
As small as fish-eggs.
The threads
Will abash him.

Third Girl
Oh, la . . . le pauvre!
I shall run before him,
With a curious puffing.
He will bend his ear then.
I shall whisper
Heavenly labials in a world of gutterals.
It will undo him.

Wallace Stevens (1879–1955), USA

stillness

25   *The soul in the garden of peace*

Meanwhile the mind, from pleasure less,
Withdraws into its happiness;
The mind, that ocean where each kind
Does straight its own resemblance find;
Yet it creates, transcending these,
Far other worlds and other seas,
Annihilating all that's made
To a green thought in a green shade.

Here at the fountain's sliding foot,
Or at some fruit tree's mossy root,
Casting the body's vest aside,
My soul into the boughs does glide:
There, like a bird, it sits and sings,
Then whets and combs its silver wings,
And, till prepared for longer flight,
Waves in its plumes the various light.

Andrew Marvell (1621–78), from "The Garden", England

26 Hermitage at Broken-Hill Monastery

Within this convent old
By the clear dawn
Tall woods are lit with earliest rays.
Lo here and there a pathway strays
On to a hidden lawn
Whose flowery thickets cells enfold.

The light upon yon hill
Lulls every bird;
And shadows on dark tarns set free
The souls of men from vanity.
Each sound of earth is still.
Only the temple bell is heard.

Ch'ang Chien (1899–1983), China

27 *Heaven-Haven*

A nun takes the veil

I have desired to go
Where springs not fail,
To fields where flies no sharp and sided hail
And a few lilies blow.

And I have asked to be
Where no storms come,
Where the green swell is in the havens dumb,
And out of the swing of the sea.

Gerard Manley Hopkins (1844–89), England

28 *Divine stillness*

Nothing in all creation is so like God as stillness.

Meister Eckhart (1260–1327), Germany

29   *Revelation*

To the mind that is still, the
whole universe surrenders.

Lao Tzu (c.604–c.531BCE) from the Tao
Te Ching, *China*

30   *Reflection*

Ah near at heart:
Far star's reflection in a well
Is still
Light.

*Kathleen Raine (b.1908), from "On a
Deserted Shore", England*

31 A quiet mind

You must strive for a quiet mind. If the eyes are perpetually restless, they cannot appreciate a beautiful object set before them; they glance this way and that, and so fail to discern the subtlety of the object's form and colour. Equally, if the mind is perpetually restless, distracted by a thousand worldly concerns, it cannot apprehend the truth.

St Basil the Great (329–79), Turkey

32 The great tree

Praise and blame, gain and loss, pleasure and sorrow come and go like the wind. To be happy, rest like a great tree in the midst of them all.

Achaan Chaa (d.1992), Thailand

33 Return to the source

Empty yourself of everything.
Let your mind be at peace.
While ten thousand things rise and fall,
    the Self contemplates their return.
Each of them grows and flourishes and
    then returns to the source.
Returning to the source is stillness,
    which is the way of nature.

Lao Tzu (c.604–c.531BCE), from the Tao Te Ching, *China*

34 Attentiveness

The no-mind state is not the vacancy of idiocy but the most supremely alert intelligence, undistracted by extraneous thought.

Ramesh Balsekar (b.1919–90), India

inner wisdom

35   *The balance of being*

You must learn to be still in the midst of activity
and to be vibrantly alive in repose.

Mahatma Gandhi (1869–1948), India

36   *Starlight*

All men have stars ... but they are not the same
things for different people. For some, who are
travellers, the stars are guides. For others, they
are no more than little lights in the sky. For others,
who are scholars, they are problems. ... But all
these stars are silent.
    You – you alone – will have the stars as no
one else has them.

Antoine de Saint-Exupéry (1900–44), France

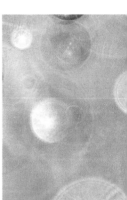

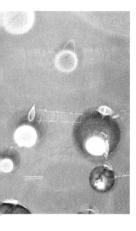

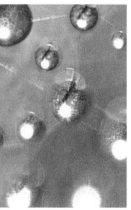

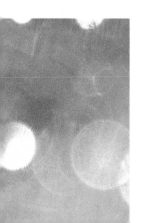

37 The mind's contribution

We must deliver ourselves with the help of our minds. ... for one who has conquered the mind, the mind is the best of friends; but for one who has failed to do so, the mind will remain the greatest enemy.

From the Bhagavad Gita *(1st–2nd century), India*

38 Peace and reason

Withdraw into your inner self. The rational principle which rules there is content with itself when it acts justly, and so maintains its own tranquillity.

Marcus Aurelius (121–80), Roman emperor

39   *Priorities*

You seek too much information and not enough transformation.

Shirdi Sai Baba (1856–1918), India

40   *Knowledge and wisdom*

Knowledge comes, but wisdom lingers.

Alfred, Lord Tennyson (1809–92), England

41   *The voice of conscience*

Conscience sometimes speaks with the voice of society,
    sometimes with the voice of the heart.
Deep in ourselves we always know the difference.

Jeanne Tardiveau (1920–94), St Lucia

42 Free will

I have given you words of vision and wisdom
more secret than hidden mysteries. Ponder
them in the silence of your soul, and then
in freedom do your will.

From the Bhagavad Gita *(1st–2nd century), India*

44 Patience

The heart is cooking
a pot of food for you.
Be patient until it is cooked.

Jalil al-Din Rumi (1207–73), Persia

43 The rule of the inner self

No one outside ourselves can rule us inwardly. When we
know this, we become free.

The Buddha (c.563–c.483BCE), India

45 The source of goodness

Dig inside. Inside is the fountain of good, and
it will forever flow, if you will forever dig.

Marcus Aurelius (121–80), Roman emperor

46 The heart's mirror

Leave all worries behind and make your heart
    totally pure, like the face of a mirror
    with no image or design.
Once your heart is cleansed of all images,
    it will contain them all.

Jalil al-Din Rumi (1207–73), Persia

giving

47   *Others*

I am in love with all the gifts of the
world, and especially those destined for
others to enjoy.

Santiago Bautista (1898–1937), Spain

48   *The good thief*

Others are my main concern.
When I notice something of mine,
I steal it and give it to others.

Shantideva (c.7th century), India

49 Simple gifts

He who offers to me with devotion only a leaf,
or a flower, or a fruit, or even a little water,
this I accept from that yearning soul, because
with a pure heart it was offered with love.

From the Bhagavad Gita *(1st–2nd century), India*

50 God's witness

You will not attain piety until you expend
part of what you love; and whatever you
expend, God knows of it.

The Koran

51   *Giving in poverty*

One must be poor to know the
luxury of giving.

George Eliot (1819–80), England

52 Showing the way

Charity is incumbent on each person every day.
Charity is assisting anyone, moving and carrying their
wares, saying a good word. Every step one takes walking
to prayer is charity. Showing the way is charity.

Muhammad (570–632)

53 A need and an ecstasy

For to the bee a flower is a fountain of life
And to the flower a bee is a messenger of love
And to both, bee and flower, the giving and the
      receiving of pleasure are a need and an ecstasy.

Kahlil Gibran (1883–1931), Lebanon

54 Energies of giving

From the infinitely changeless vessel of spirit, I savour
the inexhaustible richness of generosity.

Eduardo Cuadra (1820–1903), Chile

thankfulness

55 *Breathing*

There are two graces in breathing: drawing in air and discharging it. The former constrains, the latter refreshes: so marvellously is life mixed. Thank God then when he presses you, and thank him again when he lets you go.

Johann Wolfgang von Goethe (1749–1832), Germany

56 *The compass needle*

As a needle turns to the north when it is touched by the magnet, so it is fitting O Lord, that I, your servant, should turn to love and praise and serve you – seeing that out of love for me you were willing to endure such grievous pangs and sufferings.

Ramon Lull (1235–1315), Spain

57 Love's sweetness

Jesus, how sweet is the very thought of you! The sweetness of
your love surpasses the sweetness of honey. Nothing sweeter
than you can be described. No words can express the joy of
your love. Only those who have tasted your love for themselves
comprehend it. Thank you for giving yourself to us.

St Bernard of Clairvaux (1091–1153), France

58 The secretary

Of all the creatures both in sea and land,
Only to man thou hast made known thy ways,
And put the pen alone into his hand,
And made him secretary of thy praise.

George Herbert (1593–1633), from "Providence", England

wonder

59   *Some things ...*

Some things that fly there be
Birds – Hours – the Bumblebee –
Of these no Elegy.

Some things that stay there be –
Grief – Hills – Eternity –
Nor this behooveth me.

There are that resting, rise.
Can I expound the skies?
How still the Riddle lies!

Emily Dickinson (1830–1886), USA

60   *Wonders everywhere*

The purpose of miracles is to teach us to
see the miraculous everywhere.

St Augustine of Hippo (354–430), North Africa

61 *A string of beads*

There is a secret One inside us;
the planets in all the galaxies
pass through his hands like beads.
That is a string of beads one should look
    at with luminous eyes.

Kabir (14th century), India

62 *The wonders within*

We carry within us the wonders we seek
without us.

Sir Thomas Browne (1605–82), England

63 Being alive

Everything is extraordinarily clear. I see the whole
landscape before me, I see my hands, my feet, my
toes, and I smell the rich river mud. I feel a sense
of tremendous strangeness and wonder at being
alive. Wonder of wonders.

The Buddha (c.563–c.483BCE), India

64 The chorus of stars

You set up the sky like a canopy and spread it out
like a tent. By a mere act of will you gave the Earth
stability when there was nothing to uphold it. You
established the firmament ... and set in order the
chorus of the stars to praise your magnificence.

Eucharistic Prayer (c.380), from the Apostolic
Constitutions, *Syria*

65   *God's Grandeur*

The world is charged with the grandeur of God.
    It will flame out, like shining from shook foil;
    It gathers to a greatness, like the ooze of oil
Crushed. Why do men then now not reck his rod?
Generations have trod, have trod, have trod;
    And all is seared with trade; bleared, smeared with toil;
    And wears man's smudge and shares man's smell: the soil
Is bare now, nor can foot feel, being shod.

And for all this, nature is never spent;
    There lives the dearest freshness deep down things;
And though the last lights off the black West went
    Oh, morning, at the brown brink eastward, springs —
Because the Holy Ghost over the bent
    World broods with warm breast and with ah! bright wings.

Gerard Manley Hopkins (1844–89), England

66 A philosopher's admiration

Two things fill the mind with ever new and increasing admiration and awe, the oftener and more steadily we reflect on them: the starry heavens above and the moral law within.

Immanuel Kant (1724–1804), Germany

67 Open and closed eyes

The most beautiful thing we can experience is the mysterious. ... He to whom this emotion is a stranger – who can no longer pause to wonder and stand rapt in awe – is as good as dead: his eyes are closed.

Albert Einstein (1879–1955), Germany

68 The call of nature

The call of moon and forest was irresistible. The storms of the monsoon season also called to me. ... When I hear it now, I pause ... and I listen with awe and passion.

Thich Nhat Hanh (b.1926), Vietnam

69 Hidden depths

Our life is a faint tracing on the surface of mystery ...
"Every religion that does not affirm that God is hidden,"
said Pascal flatly, "is not true."

Annie Dillard (b.1945), USA

being in time

70 *Paradise regained*

Mindfulness helps us to regain the paradise we thought
we had lost ... If we sit firmly in the present moment, it
is as though we are sitting on a lotus.

Thich Nhat Hanh (b.1926), Vietnam

71 *The dried-up river*

The riverbed, dried-up, half-full of leaves.
Us, listening to a river in the trees.

Seamus Heaney (b.1939), epigraph to The Haw Lantern, *Ireland*

72 *The inspiration of being*

Every blade has its angel that bends over it and whispers,
"Grow, grow."

From the Talmud *(6th century)*

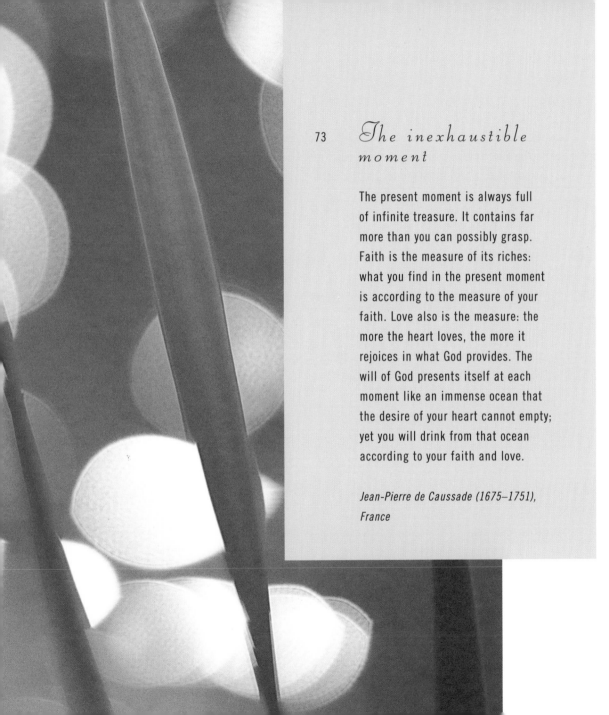

The inexhaustible moment

The present moment is always full of infinite treasure. It contains far more than you can possibly grasp. Faith is the measure of its riches: what you find in the present moment is according to the measure of your faith. Love also is the measure: the more the heart loves, the more it rejoices in what God provides. The will of God presents itself at each moment like an immense ocean that the desire of your heart cannot empty; yet you will drink from that ocean according to your faith and love.

Jean-Pierre de Caussade (1675–1751), France

74 Starting now

How wonderful it is that nobody need wait a single moment before beginning to improve the world.

Anne Frank (1929–45), Holland

75 Yesterday and tomorrow

Try to strike that delicate balance between a yesterday that should be remembered and a tomorrow that must be created.

Earl A. Grollman (20th century), USA

76 Time and ourselves

We think in eternity, but we move slowly through time.

Oscar Wilde (1854–1900), England

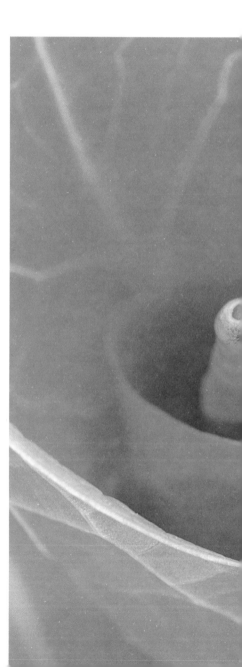

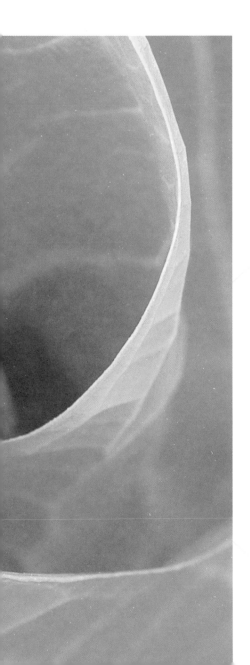

Hoping and sleeping

Put off until tomorrow those tears which fill
    your eyes and your head,
Flooding you, rolling down your cheeks, those
    tears which stream down your cheek,
Because between now and tomorrow, maybe
    I, God, will have passed your way.
Human wisdom says: Woe to the man who
    puts off what he has to do until tomorrow.
And I say: Blessed, blessed is the man who
    puts off what he has to do until tomorrow.
Blessed is he who puts off –
That is to say, Blessed is he who hopes.
    And who sleeps.

Charles Péguy (1873–1914), France

Be where you are

As you walk and eat and travel, be where you are.

Otherwise you will miss most of your life.

The Buddha (c.563–c.483BCE), India

The true dimension

Let us not look back in anger or forward in fear,
but around in awareness.

James Thurber (1894–1961), USA

I was utterly alone with the sun and the earth. Lying down on the grass,
 I spoke in my soul to the earth, the sun, the air, and the distant sea
 far beyond sight.

I thought of the earth's firmness – I felt it bear me up; through the
 grassy couch there came an influence as if I could feel the great
 earth speaking to me.

I thought of the wandering air – its pureness, which is its beauty; the air
 touched me and gave me something of itself.

I spoke to the sea: though very far, in my mind I saw it, green at the rim
 of the earth and blue in deeper ocean.

I turned to the blue heaven again, gazing into its depth, inhaling its
 exquisite colour and sweetness. The rich blue of the unattainable
 flower of the sky drew my soul towards it, and there it rested, for
 pure colour is rest of heart.

By all these I prayed.

Then, returning, I prayed by the sweet thyme, whose little flowers I
 touched with my hand; by the slender grass; by the crumble of dry
 chalky earth I took up and let fall through my fingers. Touching the
 crumble of earth, the blade of grass, the thyme flower, breathing the
 earth-encircling air, thinking of the sea and the sky, holding out my
 hand for the sunbeams to touch it, prone on the sward in token of
 deep reverence, thus I prayed.

Richard Jefferies (1848–87), England

81   The pebble

Should I now wish to examine a particular type of stone more closely,
I would choose the pebble, both because of the perfection of its form
and because I can pick it up and turn it about in my hand.

Also the pebble is stone at the exact age when personality,
individuality – in other words language – emerges.

As compared to the rockbed from which it derives directly, it is
stone already fragmented and polished into a great many almost
identical individuals. ...

While it lies there a few days longer, with no practical
significance, let us make the most of its virtues.

Francis Ponge (1899–1988), France

82   Butterflies and sunlight

I stood in a room that contained every moment –
a butterfly museum.

And the sun still as strong as before.
Its impatient brushes were painting the world.

Tomas Tranströmer (b.1931), from "Secrets on the Way", Sweden

83 The narrow gate

Every second of time is the narrow
gate through which enlightenment
might enter.

Modern inspiration from Beijing

84 Refuge

I take refuge with the Lord of the
Daybreak.

The Koran

85 The sharpness of now

The moment is what you are in. Like a sword the moment
cuts away everything around itself so that it can be free.
The sword is gentle to the touch and its edge is sharp.
Those who handle it gently are unharmed. But those who
treat it roughly are injured.

Qushayri (986–1072), from the Risalah, *Persia*

86 Initiation song

I have planted a footprint, a sacred one.
I have planted a footprint, through it the grass-blades push upward.
I have planted a footprint, through it the grass-blades radiate.
I have planted a footprint, over it the grass-blades float in the wind.
I have planted a footprint, over it I bend the stalk to pluck the ears.
I have planted a footprint, over it the blossoms lie gray.
I have planted a footprint, smoke arises from my house.
I have planted a footprint, I live in the light of day.

Anonymous (c.1900), USA

attentiveness

87   *The rain stick*

> Up-end the rain stick and what happens next
> Is a music that you never would have known
> To listen for. ...
>
> Up-end the stick again. What happens next
>
> Is undiminished for having happened once,
> Twice, ten, a thousand times before.
> Who cares if all the music that transpires
>
> Is the fall of grit or dry seeds through a cactus?
> You are like a rich man entering heaven
> Through the ear of a raindrop. Listen now again.

Seamus Heaney (b.1939), from "The Rain Stick", Ireland

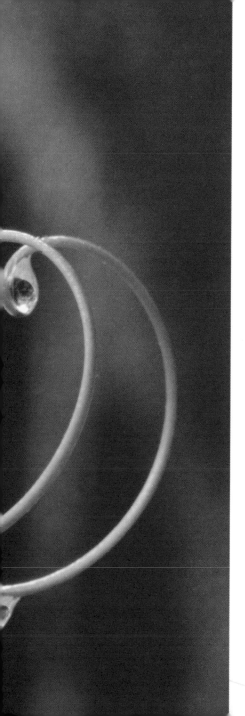

88   *Looking*

Thinking is more interesting than knowing,
but less interesting than looking.

Johann Wolfgang von Goethe (1749–1832), Germany

89   *Beyond the senses*

Our eyes believe themselves, our ears believe
other people, our intuition believes the truth
of the spirit.

Adapted from a German proverb

nature

90   *Love letters*

Everyday, priests minutely examine the Dharma
and endlessly chant complicated *sutra*s.
Before doing that, though, they should learn
how to read the love letters sent by the wind
and rain, the snow and moon.

Ikkyu (1394–1481), Japan

91   *Moon and sun*

Our cup is the full moon; our wine is the sun.

Ibn al-Farid (1181–1235), Egypt

92 *Adoration*

O never harm the dreaming world,
the world of green, the world of leaves,
but let its million palms unfold
the adoration of the trees. ...

Kathleen Raine (b.1905), from "Vegetation", England

acceptance

93   *Heaven's appointments*

The superior person is quiet and calm, waiting
patiently for Heaven's appointments. The inferior
person treads a dangerous way, always on the
look-out for good fortune.

Confucius (551–479BCE), China

94   *The universe unfolding*

You are a child of the Universe, no less than the
moon and the stars; you have a right to be here.
And whether or not it is clear to you, no doubt the
Universe is unfolding as it should.

Max Erhrmann (1872–1945), USA

95   *Love and judgment*

Abba Xanthias said: A dog is better than
I because it also has love, but it does not
pass judgment.

From the sayings of the Desert Fathers
(5th century), Egypt

96   *The educated wish*

Learn to wish that everything should come to
pass exactly as it does.

Epictetus (c.55–c.135), Greece

97 Weather wise

The gentle rain which waters my beans and keeps me in the house today is not drear and melancholy, but good for me too. Though it prevents my hoeing them, it is of far more worth than my hoeing. If it should continue so long as to cause the seeds to rot in the ground and destroy the potatoes in the low lands, it would still be good for the grass on the uplands, and, being good for the grass, it would be good for me.

Henry David Thoreau (1817–62), USA

98 The counsel of perfection

Do not seek perfection in a changing world.
Instead, perfect your love.

Master Sengstan (1911–78), China

99 Wind to willow

Willow, I have a desire to knock you over.
You bend so gracefully, so contentedly.

Grace is a wheatfield, grown from the seeds
of acceptance.

Anna Korolev (b.1960), Ukraine

100 Hold on, let go

One wears his mind out in study, and yet has more mind
with which to study. One gives away his heart in love and
yet has more heart to give away. One perishes out of pity
for a suffering world, and is stronger therefore. So, too,
it is possible at one and the same time to hold on to
life and let go.

Milton Steinberg (d.1950), USA

simplicity

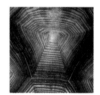

101 The ego and the self

Like two golden birds perched on a tree,
the ego and the self are united companions:
one eats the sweet and sour fruits of the tree,
while the other looks on without eating.
As long as you identify with the ego,
you will feel attached to both joy and sorrow.
But if you know that you are the self, the lord of life,
you will be freed from suffering.
You will transcend duality
and move into a state of Oneness.

From the Bhagavad Gita *(6th century BCE), India*

102 A pot and its purpose

The usefulness of a pot comes from its emptiness.

Lao Tzu (c.604–c.531BCE), from the Tao Te Ching, *China*

103   *Be like the tortoise*

When one withdraws all desires as a
tortoise withdraws its limbs, then the
natural splendour of the world soon
manifests itself.

From the Mahabharata *(c.400ʙᴄᴇ–c.200ᴄᴇ), India*

104   *Enough*

I think that maybe
I will be a little surer
of being a little nearer.
That is all. Eternity
is in the understanding
that little is more than enough.

R. S. Thomas (b.1913), Wales

In the end these things matter most: How well did you love? How fully did you love? How deeply did you learn to let go?

The Buddha (c.563–c.483BCE), India

106 *Eternity*

He who binds to himself a joy

Does the winged life destroy;

But he who kisses the joy as it flies

Lives in eternity's sun rise.

William Blake (1757–1822), England

happiness

107 The rest of joy

The Holy Spirit does not rest where there is idleness, or sadness, or ribaldry, or frivolity, or empty speech. But only where there is joy.

From the Midrash Psalms *(c.2nd century)*

108 Mother's song

it's quiet in the house so quiet
outside the snowstorm wails
the dogs curl up noses under their tails
my little son sleeps on his back
his mouth open
his belly rises and falls
breathing
is it strange if I cry for joy?

Anonymous (19th century), translated from the Inuit

109 Source of contentment

Beauty remains even in misfortune. If you just look for it, you discover more and more happiness and regain your balance. A person who's happy will make others happy; a person who has courage will never die in misery.

Anne Frank (1929–45), Holland

110 The door

The door of happiness does not open away from us: we cannot rush at it to push it open. It opens toward us and, therefore, nothing is required of us.

Søren Kierkegaard (1813–55), Denmark

111 *You and your shadow*

Speak or act with a pure mind, and happiness will follow you as your shadow, unshakable.

The Buddha (c.563–c.483BCE), India

True contentment

Happiness is found on the familiar highways of life; contentment is a herb that grows very close to the earth.

Melville Harcourt (b.1909), USA

truth

113   *The law of truth and love*

Those who know the truth are not equal to those who love the truth.

Confucius (551–479BCE), China

114   The gaze toward truth

Those who love truth more than life itself turn away from the fleeting things of time with all their souls. To use an expression of Plato – God himself sets their faces in the right direction.

Simone Weil (1909–43), France

115 The self in truth's embrace

If you would swim
on the bosom
of the ocean of Truth,
you must reduce
yourself to a zero.

Mahatma Gandhi (1869–1948), India

116 Reason in its place

Lord, help me never to use my reason against the Truth.

Jewish prayer

117 *Each of us*

Truth exists only for each individual

when he produces it through his actions.

Søren Kierkegaard (1813–55), Denmark

Not everyone can see the truth,

but everyone can *be* the truth.

Franz Kafka (1883–1924), Austria

wordlessness

119   ## The rule of moonlight

Close the language-door,
and open the love-window.

The moon won't use the door,
only the window.

Jalil al-Din Rumi (1307–87), Persia

120   ## Before you speak ...

Before you speak, ask yourself:
is it kind, is it necessary,
is it true, does it improve on the silence?

Shirdi Sai Baba (1856–1918), India

The scent of the rose

Rose, we are your coronation. To the ancients
you were a pale cup with a simple rim.
Now to us you are the infinite concordance
of spirit unfolding – *Rosa seriatim*.

In your opulence you seem to be wearing gown
upon gown on a body of nothing but light –
yet each petal separately appears to disown
and dissolve all dress in its endless midnight.

Your fragrance has whispered name after name
to us across the void for centuries.
Again, suddenly, it hangs in the air like fame,

yet still the words escape us. Perhaps we've guessed ...
but all we live for is to open our memories
to that sweetness, and the hours it laid to rest.

after Rainer Maria Rilke (1875–1926), Austria
(seriatim: in a series, one after the other)

122 *An awakening*

The word is fast asleep under the blanket of the adjective. Shall I wake it up?

Labshankar Thacker (b.1935), India

123 *Earth*

It's wonderful to think

Of such a long river

With no words in it.

Haiku by Jay Ramsay (20th century), England

humility

124 Flying toward the sun

Lord Jesus, I am not an eagle.
All I have are the eyes and
the heart of one. In spite of my littleness,
I dare to gaze at the sun of love,
and I long to fly toward it.

St Thérèse of Lisieux (1873–97), France

125 An old man's advice

A brother asked an old man: "What is humility?" And the old
man said: "To do good to those who hurt you." The brother said:
"If you cannot go that far, what should you do?" The old man
replied: "Get away from them and keep your mouth shut".

From the sayings of the Desert Fathers (5th century), Egypt

126   *Soul house*

I am not worthy, Master and Lord, that you should come beneath the
roof of my soul; yet since in your love toward all, you wish to dwell
in me, in boldness I come. You command, open the gates, which you
alone have made. And you will come in, and enlighten my darkened
reasoning. I believe that you will do this, for you did not send away
that harlot who came to you with tears, nor cast out the repenting
tax-collector, nor reject the thief who acknowledged your kingdom.
But you counted all of these as members of your band of friends.
You are blessed evermore.

St John Chrysostom (c.347–c.407), Turkey

127   *Self-assessment*

The Sage knows himself, but does not show himself.
He loves himself but does not value himself.

Lao Tzu (c.604–c.531BCE), from the Tao Te Ching, *China*

By contrast

Humility like darkness reveals the heavenly lights.

Henry David Thoreau (1817–62), USA

fit to be a pilgrim

Would you be a pilgrim on the road to Love?

The first condition is that you make yourself

as humble as dust and ashes.

Ansari of Herat (1066–89)

faith

130 *Night walk*

If a man wishes to be sure of the road he treads on,
he must close his eyes and walk in the dark.

St John of the Cross (1542–91), Spain

131 *The flight of beauty*

Ah –
I patiently close my eyes on all the grins and smirks,
on all the twisted smiles and horse laughs –
and glimpse then, inside me,
one beautiful white butterfly
fluttering toward tomorrow.

*Kuroda Saburo (20th century), from
"I Am Completely Different", Japan*

132   *Immunity*

Belief is better than anything else, and it is best when rapt – above paying its respects to anybody's doubt whatsoever.

Robert Frost (1874–1963), USA

133   *Wonders unseen*

Keep your faith in beautiful things; in the sun when it is hidden, in the Spring when it is gone.

Roy R. Gibson (20th century), USA

134 El hombre

It's a strange courage
you give me ancient star:

Shine alone in the sunrise
toward which you lend no part!

William Carlos Williams (1883–1963), USA

135 Windows

He to whom worshipping is a window,
    to open but also to shut, has not
yet visited the house of his soul whose
    windows are open from dawn to dawn.

Kahlil Gibran (1883–1931), Lebanon

136 Night as day

If I take the wings of the morning and settle at
    the farthest limits of the sea,
even there your hand shall lead me, and your
    right hand shall hold me fast.
If I say, "Surely the darkness shall cover me,
    and the light around me become night,"
even the darkness is not dark to you; the night
    is as bright as the day, for darkness is as
    light to you.

Psalm *139:9–12*

137 The thirsty fish

I laugh when I hear that the fish in the water is thirsty.
I laugh when I hear that men go on pilgrimage to find God.

Kabir (15th century), India

God's children

Beloved, we are God's children now; what we will be has not yet been revealed. What we do know is this: when he is revealed, we will be like him, for we will see him as he is.

1 John *3:2*

Faith begins where imagination ends.

Søren Kierkegaard (1813–55), Denmark

140 A fountain of leaves

Deliver us from the long drought of the mind;
Let leaves from the deciduous cross fall on us
Washing us clean
Turning our autumn to gold
By the affluence of their fountain.

R.S. Thomas (1913–2000), Wales

141 Everywhere the divine

God to surround me, God to encompass me;
God in my words, God in my thoughts;
God in my waking, God in my resting;
God in my hoping, God in my doing;
God in my heart, God in my soul;
God in my weakness, God in my strength;
God in my life, God in my eternity;
God in my life, God in my eternity.

W. Mary Calvert (20th century), USA

142 Shining faith

No coward soul is mine,
No trembler in the world's storm-troubled sphere.
I see Heaven's glories shine,
And Faith shines equal, arming me from Fear.

Emily Brontë (1818–48), from "No Coward Soul is Mine", England

143 The fountain of life

How precious is your steadfast love, O God!
    All people may take refuge in the shadow of your wings.
They feast on the abundance of your house,
    and you give them drink from the river of your delights.
For with you is the fountain of life;
    in your light we see light.

Psalm *36:7–9*

Never put anyone out of your heart ...

Maharaj-ji (c.1890–1973), India

The inner circle of love

• Empathy • Selflessness • Compassion
• Friendship • Family • Karma • Everyday Love
• Sacred Union • Mystic Love • Partings • New Life

empathy

145 Another's soul

What have we seen of another person, when the shutters of the soul are closed? About as much as the cover of a book.

Sten Stensen Blicher (1728–1848), Denmark

146 The secret history

If we could read the secret history of our enemies we should find in each man's life sorrow and suffering enough to disarm all hostility.

Henry Wadsworth Longfellow (1807–82), USA

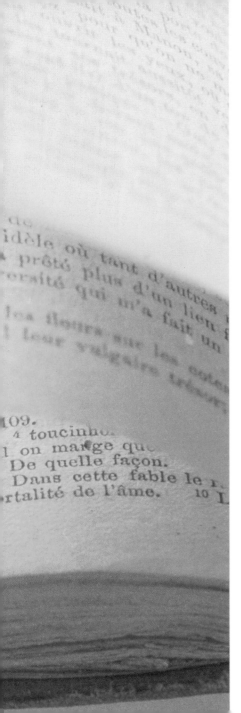

147 Comparisons

Use all your faculties to appreciate God's love.
Use your soul to understand other souls. Use
your body to sympathize with other people's
bodily experiences. Use your emotions of anger
and revenge to understand war. Appreciate
goodness by distinguishing it from evil. Enjoy
every moment of life by constantly reminding
yourself of the imminence of death.

St Hildegard von Bingen (1098–1179), Germany

148 Healing wounds

Our hearts are healthy in a sick way when we are
not wounded by God's love. ... But they are wounded
to be healed when God strikes insensible minds
with the barbs of his love and soon renders them
sensitive through the fire of charity.

St Gregory the Great (c.540–c.604), Rome

selflessness

149 Others' happiness

All happiness comes from the desire for
    others to be happy.
All misery comes from the desire for oneself
    to be happy.

Shantideva (c.7th century), India

150 How to be brothers

None of you is a true believer until you wish
for your brother what you wish for yourself.

*From the Hadith (c.7th century), the spoken Islamic
tradition attributed to the Prophet Muhammad*

151 *True giving*

The only gift is a portion of thyself.

Ralph Waldo Emerson (1803–82), USA

152 *The story of the sandals*

One day Rabbi Tarfan's mother's sandals split and
broke, and as she could not mend them, she had to
walk across the courtyard barefoot. So Rabbi Tarfan
kept stretching his hands under her feet, so that she
might walk over them, all the way.

From the Talmud *(6th century)*

153 *Transcendence*

To be selfless is to be all-pervading.

To be all-pervading is to be transcendent.

Lao Tzu (c.604–c.531BCE), from the Tao Te Ching, *China*

I will cease to live as a self and will take as my self my fellow-creatures.

Shantideva (c.7th century), India

compassion

155 *A promise*

They whose minds
are filled with kindness
will never enter
a world dark with woes.

Tiruvalluvar (c.1st century BCE), India

156 *The trance of compassion*

By practicing kindness all over with everyone you will soon come
into the holy trance, definite distinctions of personalities will
become what they really mysteriously are, our common and eternal
blissstuff, the pureness of everything forever, the great bright
essence of mind, even and one thing everywhere the holy eternal
milky love, the white light everywhere everything, emptybliss, svaha,
shining, ready, and awake, the compassion in the sound of silence,
the swarming myriad trillionaire you are.

Jack Kerouac (1923–1969), USA

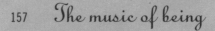

The music of being

We can be spacious yet full of loving kindness; full of compassion, yet serene. Live like the strings of a fine instrument — not too taut but not too loose.

The Buddha (c.563–c.483BCE), India

A duty

The first duty of love is to listen.

Paul Tillich (1886–1965), USA

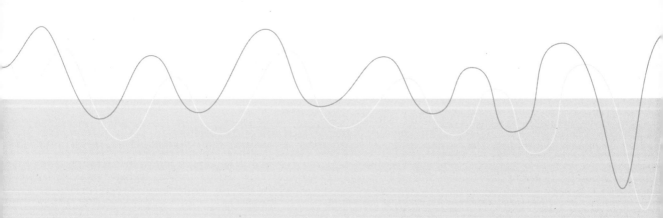

Listen, or your tongue will keep you deaf.

Native North American proverb

160 Strength of feeling

True compassion flows fast, as if we were wounded ourselves, yet without diminishing our strength.

Modern inspiration from Tokyo

161 The chain of love

You shall not enter Paradise until you have faith, and you cannot have faith until you love one another. Have compassion on those you can see, and He whom you cannot see will have compassion on you.

From the Hadith *(c.7th century), the spoken Islamic tradition attributed to the Prophet Muhammad*

162   *A noble soul*

A superior being does not render evil for evil.
Never harm the wicked or the good or even
criminals meriting death. A noble soul is always
compassionate, even toward those who enjoy
injuring others or who are actually committing
cruel deeds – for who is without fault?

From the Ramayana *(c.300BCE), India*

163   *Parents*

It is the way of a father to be compassionate and
it is the way of a mother to comfort. The Holy One
said: "I will act like a father and a mother."

Pesikta de-Rav Kahana *19:3 (c.2nd century), India*

164 Dimensions

"And behold a wall on the outside of the house round about, and in the man's hand a measuring reed of six cubits long by the cubit and a hand breadth: so he measured the breadth of the building, one reed; and the height, one reed." Ezekiel 40:5

Breadth pertains to charity for the neighbour; height to the understanding of the Maker. The breadth and the height of the building are measured at one cubit because each soul will be as high in knowledge of God as it is broad in love of neighbour. While it enlarges itself in width through love, it lifts itself in height through knowledge, and it is as high above itself as it extends outside itself in love of neighbour.

St Gregory the Great (c.540–c.604), Rome

165 *The sick room*

I turn with love my face to your sickness.
If one atom of my heart shows a squeamish impulse to run away,
    let it be said I am less whole than you.
I turn with love my face and loving touch
    to ease your sickness and give thanks for your courage.
Let my closeness be my prayer for your renewal.

Maria Glauber (b.1953), Germany

166 *Ends, not means*

Act in such a way that you always treat humanity, whether in your
own person or in the person of any other, never simply as a means,
but always at the same time as an end.

Immanuel Kant (1724–1804), Germany

friendship

167 *The heart's morning*

And in the sweetness of friendship let there
be laughter, and sharing of pleasure,
For in the dew of little things the heart finds
its morning and is refreshed.

Kahlil Gibran (1883–1931), Lebanon

168 *Gold*

How will you know your real friends?
Pain is as dear to them as life.
A friend is like gold. Trouble is like fire.
Pure gold delights in the fire.

Jalil al-Din Rumi (1307–87), Persia

169 *Such love ...*

Such love I cannot analyse;
It does not rest in lips or eyes,
Neither in kisses nor caress.
Partly, I know, it's gentleness

And understanding in one word
Or in brief letters. It's preserved
By trust and by respect and awe.
These are the words I'm feeling for.

Elizabeth Jennings (1926–2001), from
"Friendship", England

170 *Maturing*

A new friend is new wine;
When it grows old, you will enjoy drinking it.

Ben Sira (c.2nd century BCE), Israel

171 *Mirror and window*

Friend, be my mirror,
    tell me when I do wrong, or if you are too kind,
    let my failings show up in the frame of all your virtues.

Friend, be my window,
    convince me that I live in a small cell of habit.
    I long to join you on the endless frontier of your openness.

Lourdes Mallo (b.1930), Gran Canaria

172 *Enrichment*

Always seek out friends who are
wise, and perhaps a little on the
rigorous side – such company will
be spiritually enriching.

Otto Rix (1820–1903), Vienna

173 The shell of friendship

The reflection cast from good friends is needed
until you become with the aid of any reflector,
    a drawer of water from the Sea.
Know that the reflection is at first just imitation,
    but when it continues to recur,
    it turns into direct realization of truth.
Until it has become realization,
don't part from the friends who guide you —
    don't break away from the shell
    if the raindrop hasn't yet become a pearl.

Jalil al-Din Rumi (1307–87), Persia

174 Silent companionship

If friendship is firmly established
between two hearts, they do not need
to exchange news.

Sa'ib of Tabriz (c.1601–77), Persia

175 Significant hours

I always think that we live, spiritually, by
what others have given us in the significant
hours of our life. These significant hours do
not announce themselves as coming, but
arrive unexpected.

Albert Schweitzer (1875–1965), France

176 All but a bird

Friendship is Love without his wing.

Lord Byron (1788–1824), England

177 The rule of three

Friendship with the virtuous, friendship
with the sincere, friendship with the
observant – these three friendships
are advantageous.

Confucius (551–479BCE), China

family

178 *The gift of civilization*

I must study politics and war, that my sons
may have the liberty to study mathematics and
philosophy, geography, natural history, and
naval architecture, navigation, commerce,
and agriculture, in order to give their children
a right to study painting, poetry, music,
architecture, statuary, tapestry and porcelain.

John Quincy Adams (1767–1848), USA

179 *Question and answer*

What is the best thing I can do for you, my children?
Love yourself and love our mother.

Joann Hertzberger (1899–1960), Holland

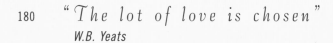

180　　"*The lot of love is chosen*"
W.B. Yeats

But do you choose, or else does love choose you?
Our common speech, that utters mysteries
Only half known, insists we *fall* in love.
Who voyages on those seas
Goes to the ends of the world, a lifetime's journey.
Yet vows are chosen, and acts that make them good
Chosen, for better, for worse, or hard or easy.

I search for words to bless you, find none right,
But see that you from stores of joy already
Are blessing others, while your joys increase.
Blest be your chosen lot, dear son and daughter,
And the journey you began before you willed it –
Falling in love – upon those passionate seas.

Anne Ridler (1912–2001), England

181 A wish for my children

On this doorstep I stand
year after year
and watch you leaving

and think: May you not
skin your knees. May you
not catch your fingers
in car doors. May
your hearts not break.

May tide and weather
wait for your coming

and may you grow strong
to break
all webs of my weaving.

Evangeline Paterson (d.2000), England

182 Another way

Don't limit a child to your own way of loving,
for he was born in another time.

Adapted from a Rabbinical saying

183 Growing up

When I asked you as a child
How high should fences be
To keep in the butterflies,
Blood was already passing
Down median and margin
To the apex of a wing.

*Michael Longley (b.1939), from "The
White Butterfly", Northern Ireland*

184 *Forever young*

Youth never disappears, for it is still in harmony with
the Divine.

Alexandre Dumas (1824–95), France

185 *The flag of love*

Our son and daughter treasure the tattered flag of our love.
This banner survived their revolution.
Threadbare now, it has become unutterably precious.
Like embers, it glows with familial warmth whenever their
    breath comes close enough.
We know that one day its threads and colors will be bathed
    in the renewing spring of a grandchild's cry for freedom.

Esther Cohen (b.1971), USA

186 *Your children ...*

Your children are not your children.
They are sons and daughters of life's longing for itself.
They come through you but not from you,
And though they are with you, yet they belong not to you.
You may give them your love but not your thoughts
For they have their own thoughts.

You may house their bodies but not their souls,
For their souls dwell in the house of tomorrow, which you
    cannot visit, not even in your dreams.
You may strive to be like them, but seek not to make
    them like you.
For life goes not backward nor tarries with yesterday.

Kahlil Gibran (1883–1935), Lebanon

karma

187   *Your shadow*

Rise up to the heavens or move to the ends
of the world, plunge into the deep sea or
stay where you are: the consequences of
works that bring fortune and misfortune to
people, accumulated in previous lives, will
follow you like a shadow.

Sahityadarpana 3:21 (c.14th century), India

188   *Obligation*

We have no more right to consume happiness without producing
it than to consume wealth without producing it.

George Bernard Shaw (1856–1950), Ireland

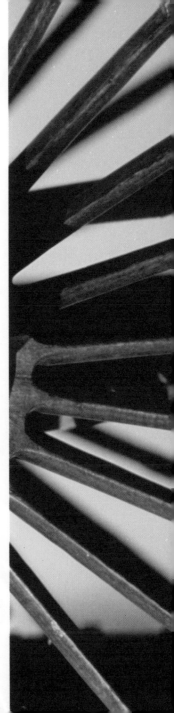

189 The rule of returns

Whoever gives reverence receives reverence:
whoever brings sugar eats almond cake.

Jalil al-Din Rumi (1307–87), Persia

190 On two wheels

The success of one's actions rests equally
on destiny and on personal effort. Destiny
is the fruit of efforts made in a previous
life. As a chariot cannot move on one
wheel alone, so without personal effort
destiny alone accomplishes nothing.

Yajnavalkyasmriti 1:349–53, India

191 Nourishment

The reward for a good deed performed in this world will be enjoyed in the next world; when one waters the roots of trees, fruits form at their branches.

Subhashitarnava *271, India*

192 Light and dark

There are two ways of passing from this world – one in light and one in darkness. Someone who passes in light does not come back; but someone who passes in darkness returns.

From the Bhagavad Gita *(1st–2nd century), India*

193 Lifesavers

Whoever saves one life, it is as if he saved the entire world.

From the Talmud *(6th century)*

194 The sword

Then Jesus said to him, "Put your sword back into its place; for all those who take the sword will perish by the sword. ..."

Matthew *26:52*

everyday love

195   *Love in daily use*

And here is love
like a tinsmith's scoop
sunk past its gleam
in the meal-bin.

Seamus Heaney (b.1939) from "Mossbawn:
Two Poems in Dedication", Ireland

196 *Work and wind*

My fine strong horse
can pull a heavy plough
and never tire.

Yet it can also gallop
through a wild country.

I am working hard at love,
with the wind in my hair.

José Morazán (b.1952), Honduras

By day and night

Togetherness: to pray together by day in blessed harness, and rest together by night in mystic peace.

Juliana Pereira (1895–1976), Lisbon

198 *A shelter for solitude*

I hold this to be the highest task for a bond between two people, that each protects the solitude of the other.

Rainer Maria Rilke (1875–1926), Austria

199 Harmony

Stand off from me; be still your own;
Love's perfect chord maintains the sense
Through harmony, not unison,
Of finest difference.

Edward Dowden (1843–1913), from "Love's Chord", Ireland

200 Beyond the reflection

The beginning of love is to let those we
love be perfectly themselves, and not to
twist them to fit our own image. Otherwise
we love only the reflection of ourselves
we find in them.

Thomas Merton (1915–68), USA

201 Side by side

Life has taught me that love does not consist
in gazing at each other but in looking outward
together in the same direction.

Antoine de Saint-Exupéry (1900–44), France

202 Letting go

We need in love to practise only this:
letting each other go. For holding on comes
easily — we do not need to learn it.

Rainer Maria Rilke (1875–1926), Austria

203 *Revelations*

There is nothing that will not reveal its
secrets if you love it enough.

George Washington Carver (1864–1943), USA

204 *Seeing things anew*

I am the silk page at your fingertips
running down on me, the fruit you revolve
and leave mapped in bloom, the blur of a lens
you lift a shirt hem to, rub over, breathe on,
I am the way you see the world anew.

Mimi Khalvati (b.1944), from "Tenderness",
England

205 *The philosophy of love*

Good is the magnetic centre towards which love
naturally moves. False love moves to false good. False
love embraces false death. When true good is loved,
even impurely or by accident, the quality of the love
is automatically refined, and when the soul is turned
towards Good the highest part of the soul is enlivened.
Love is the tension between the imperfect soul and the
magnetic perfection which is conceived of as lying
beyond it. ... And when we try perfectly to love what is
imperfect our love goes to its object *via* the Good to be
thus purified and made unselfish and just. ... Love is
the general name of the quality of attachment and it
is capable of infinite degradation and is the source
of our greatest errors; but when it is even partially
refined it is the energy and passion of the soul in its
search for Good, the force that joins us to Good and
joins us to the world through Good. Its existence is the
unmistakable sign that we are spiritual creatures,
attracted by excellence and made for the Good. It is
a reflection of the warmth and light of the sun.

Iris Murdoch (1919–99), England

206 Resistance

Let us love the country of here below.
It is real; it offers resistance to love.

Simone Weil (1909–43), France

207 Working with love

And what is it to work with love?
It is to weave the cloth with threads drawn
    from your heart, even as if your beloved
    were to wear that cloth.
It is to build a house with affection, even as
    if your beloved were to dwell in that house.
It is to sow seeds with tenderness and reap
    the harvest with joy, even as if your
    beloved were to eat the fruit.

Kahlil Gibran (1833–1931), Lebanon

208 *The challenge*

For one human being to love another: that is
perhaps the most difficult of all our tasks,
the ultimate, the last test and proof, the work
for which all other work is but preparation.

Rainer Maria Rilke (1875–1926), Austria

209 *A moonlit night*

There is a way from your heart to mine
and my heart knows it,
because it is clean and pure like water.
When the water is still like a mirror,
it can behold the Moon.

Jalil al-Din Rumi (1307–87), Persia

sacred union

210 *Wonder in my heart*

... here is the deepest secret nobody knows
(here is the root of the root and the bud of the bud
and the sky of the sky of a tree called life; which
grows higher than the soul can hope or mind can
hide) and this is the wonder that's keeping the stars
apart i carry your heart(i carry it in my heart) ...

*E.E. Cummings (1894–1962), from "i carry your heart
with me(i carry it in", USA*

211 Blessing for a lover

You are the star of each night,
You are the brightness of every morning,
You are the story of each guest
You are the report of every land.

No evil shall befall you. On hill or bank,
In field or valley. On mountain or in glen.

Neither above nor below. Neither in sea
Nor on shore,
In skies above. Nor in the depths.

You are the kernel of my heart,
You are the face of my sun,
You are the harp of my music,
You are the crown of my company.

Modern Celtic blessing from Ireland

212 As I dig for wild orchids

As I dig for wild orchids
in the autumn fields,
it is the deeply-bedded root
that I desire,
not the flower.

Izumi Shikibu (c.974–c.1034), Japan

213 For a wedding

This is the chaste kiss of our union:
    for one miraculous moment
    all nature is our congregation and our choir.
We have the ear and eye of heaven.
The One smiles in our hearts.

No moment could be more sacred in our lives.
    We rejoice that we are thought worthy to be
    actors in the peaceful drama of blissful souls.
We have the hope and courage of heaven.
The One smiles in our hearts.

Manon Williams (1920–2001), Wales

214 Soulmates

Heart, are you great enough
    For a love that never tires?
O heart, are you great enough for love?
I have a heart of thorns and briers.
Over the thorns and briers,
    Over the meadows and stiles,
Over the world to the end of it
    Flash for a million miles.

Alfred, Lord Tennyson (1809-92), from
"Marriage Morning", England

215 *On marriage*

Then Almitra spoke again and said, And what of Marriage, master?
And he answered saying:
You were born together, and together you shall be for evermore.
You shall be together when the white wings of death scatter your days,
Ay, you shall be together even in the silent memory of God.
But let there be spaces in your togetherness,
And let the winds of the heavens dance between you.

Give your hearts, but not into each other's keeping.
For only the hand of life can contain your hearts.
And stand together yet not too near together:
For the pillars of the temple stand apart,
And the oak tree and the cypress grow not in each other's shadow.

Kahlil Gibran (1883–1931), Lebanon

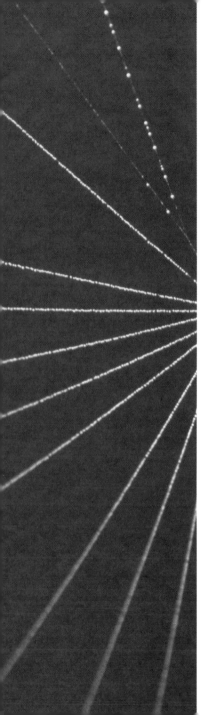

mystic love

216   *Eternal fire*

But true love is a durable fire
In the mind ever burning;
Never sick, never old, never dead,
From itself never turning.

*Walter Raleigh (c.1552–1618) from "As Ye Came
from the Holy Land of Walsinghame", England*

217   *King Solomon's wedding*

King Solomon made himself a chariot of the wood of
Lebanon.

He made the pillars thereof of silver, the bottom thereof
of gold, the covering of it of purple, the midst thereof being
paved with love, for the daughters of Jerusalem.

Go forth, O ye daughters of Zion, and behold King
Solomon with the crown wherewith his mother crowned him
in the day of his espousals, and in the day of the gladness
of his heart.

Song of Solomon *3:9–11*

218 The halo

My soul gave me good counsel, teaching me to love.
Love was for me a delicate thread stretched between
two adjacent pegs, but now it has been transformed
into a halo; its first is its last, and its last is its first.
It encompasses every being, slowly expanding to
embrace all that ever will be.

Jalil al-Din Rumi (1307–87), Persia

219 The peace you bring

And for what, except for you, do I feel love?
Do I press the extremest book of the wisest man
Close to me, hidden in me day and night?
In the uncertain light of single, certain truth,
Equal in living changingness to the light
In which I meet you, in which we sit at rest,
For a moment in the central of our being,
The vivid transparence that you bring is peace.

*Wallace Stevens (1879–1955), prologue to "Notes
Toward a Supreme Fiction", USA*

220 *Love's beauty*

Were I to promise love in a hundred thousand languages,
love's beauty far surpasses all such stammerings.

Jalil al-Din Rumi (1307–87), Persia

Love turns a battery of stings into a paradise of honey.

Love sets the slave on a golden throne.

Modern inspiration from Turkey

222 Perfect vision

"If I glow on thee with the flame of love
beyond all that is seen on earth so that
I overcome the power of thine eyes, do not
marvel, for it comes from perfect vision,
which, as it apprehends, moves towards
the apprehended good. I see well how there
shines now in thy mind the eternal light
which, seen, alone and always kindles
love; and if aught else beguile your love
it is nothing but some trace of this,
ill-understood, that shines through thee."

Dante Alighieri (1265–1321), Paradiso, *Canto V*
(Beatrice addressing Dante), Italy

223 *His music*

I am in love and want the world to see.
I have carved the many names of God
    onto all the trees
within the sacred grove of my heart
    from which His music plays.

I am in love and want the world to hear.
I have no doubt His music will charm
    tiger and lion, snake and bullet ant,
disarm logger and poacher,
    bandit and tax collector.

From a folk song, Senegal

224 *The astrolabe of God's mysteries*

The lover's ailment is not like any other;
Love is the astrolabe of God's mysteries.
Whether Love is from heaven or earth,
    it points to God.

Jalil al-Din Rumi (1307–87), Persia

225 Union

In so far as love is union, it knows no extremes of distance.

Juana Ines de la Cruz (1651–95), Mexico

226 Beyond the mind

Go to the truth beyond the mind. Love is the bridge.

Stephen Levine (20th century), USA

227 *The kiss of peace*

Love overflows into all:
From the glorious ocean's depths
    to beyond the farthest star,
Bounteous in loving all creation;
For to the King most High
Love has given her kiss of peace.

St Hildegard von Bingen (1098–1179),
Germany

partings

228   *Landscapes*

Watching the distant darkening hills, the trees bending
with the black weight of your absence, I think of you ...
and you are always with me, watching the clouds hurry over
the dangerous waking seas, the islands biding their time
like whales. Let us smile together, safe in our love that
conquers distance, contented even in the bleak landscapes
of separation.

Paolo Marinetti (1799–1853), Italy

229   *Reserves of sweetness*

Now we must draw, as plants would,
On tubers stored in a better season,
Our honey and heaven;
Only our love can store such food.

Anne Ridler (1912–2001), from "At Parting", England

230   With my blessing

You're leaving me. Then go in peace. And let
Your wish alone be lamp to light your path,
And find tranquillity where'er you be.

*Chaim Nachman Bialik (1873–1934), from "You're
Leaving Me", Israel*

new life

231   *The everyday miracle*

When people truly open their minds, and
contemplate the way in which the universe
is ordered and governed, they are amazed —
overwhelmed by a sense of the miraculous.
When people contemplate with open minds
the germination of a single seed, they are
equally overwhelmed — yet numerous babies
are born every day, and no-one marvels. If
only people opened their minds, they would
see that the birth of a baby, in which a new
life is created, is a greater miracle than
restoring life.

St Augustine of Hippo (354–430), North Africa

The catalyst

Long after the birth,
she held up the X-ray
of her second-born son
in the womb.

There he hung
against the light,
head-down to the lintel,
translucent
as wax in a glass.

What she saw
was not simply
the curve of the spine,
the seal at the cervix,

but sacrament brightly stilled;
an angelical stone
that cannot be weighed;

the catalyst
of sun through wax –
the ghostly body –
at the casual supper
Christ eating the honeycomb.

Pauline Stainer (b.1941), England

233 Greeting the world

Long time before
I in my mother's womb was born,
A God preparing did this glorious store,
The world, for me adorn.
Into this Eden so divine and fair,
So wide and bright, I come His son
and heir.

A stranger here
Strange things doth meet, strange
glories see;
Strange treasures lodged in this fair
world appear,
Strange all, and new to me.
But that they mine should be, who
nothing was,
That strangest is of all, yet brought
to pass.

*Thomas Traherne (1637–74), from "The
Salutation", England*

234 Clouds of glory

Our birth is but a sleep and a forgetting:
The soul that rises with us, our life's star,
Hath had elsewhere its setting,
And cometh from afar:
Not in entire forgetfulness,
And not in utter nakedness,
But trailing clouds of glory do we come
From God, who is our home:
Heaven lies about us in our infancy!

*William Wordsworth (1770–1850), from
"Ode: Intimations of Immortality", England*

235   *For a new-born child*

Blessing, sleep and grow taller in sleeping.
Lie ever in kind keeping.
Infants curl in a cowrie of peace
And should lie lazy. After this ease,
When the soul out of its safe shell goes,
Stretched as you stretch those knees and toes,
What should I wish you? Intelligence first,
In a credulous age by instruction cursed.
Take from us both what immunity
We have from the germ of the printed lie.
Your father's calm temper I wish you, and
The shaping power of his confident hand.
Much, too, that is different and your own;
And may we learn to leave you alone.
For your part, forgive us the pain of living,
Grow in that harsh sun great-hearted and loving.

Anne Ridler (1912–2001), from "For a Christening", England

236 *The seed*

The greatest dreams on Earth

I trust to you my child.

You are the seed of humankind,

the hope, the future of the world.

Trán Düc Uyén (20th century), from "A Letter to My Future Child", Vietnam

The living yes

As I am innocent, everything I do

Or say is couched in the affirmative.

Derek Mahon, (b.1941) from "An Unborn Child", Ireland

238 *Fully alive*

I will not die an unlived life.
I will not live in fear
of falling or catching fire.
I choose to inhabit my days,
to allow my living to open me,
to make me less afraid,
more accessible,
to loosen my heart until it becomes a wing,
a torch, a promise.
I choose to risk my significance;
to live so that which came to me as seed
goes to the next as blossom
and that which came to me as blossom,
goes on as fruit.

Dawna Markova (20th century), USA

239 A difficult joy

For birth is awaking, birth is effort and pain;
And now at midwinter are the hints, inklings
(Sodden primrose, honeysuckle greening)
That sleep must be broken.
To bear new life or learn to live is an exacting joy:
The whole self must waken; you cannot predict the way
It will happen, or master the responses beforehand.

Anne Ridler (1912–2001), from "Christmas and Common Birth", England

240 A child asleep in its own life

Among the old men that you know,
There is one, unnamed, that broods
On all the rest, in heavy thought.

They are nothing, except in the universe
Of that single mind. He regards them
Outwardly and knows them inwardly,

The sole emperor of what they are,
Distant, yet close enough to wake
The chords above your bed to-night.

Wallace Stevens (1879–1955), USA

After the life and the dream
comes what matters most:
the awakening.

Don Paterson (b.1963), after Antonio Machado
(1875–1939), Spain

The outer circle of spirit

in times of darkness

242 Fragrant love

Wine sweetened with honey is used
to pacify bees – When the bees smell
this pungent and pleasant odour, they
become peaceful; they sit quietly,
relishing the fragrance. Similarly,
when our hearts are in turmoil, God
pours his spiritual wine into us – and
all the warring powers of the soul fall
into a delightful repose. We feel and
sense nothing except the fragrance
of God's love – we simply enjoy God.

Francis de Sales (1567–1622), France

243 Acceptance

If you are irritated by every rub,
how will your mirror be polished?

Jalil al-Din Rumi (1207–73), Persia

244 Troubled shores

A great man does not lose his self-possession
when he is afflicted; the ocean is not made
muddy by the falling of its banks.

From the Panchatantra *(6th century), India*

245 The dark night of the soul

Even though the night darkens your spirit,
its purpose is to impart light. Even though
it humbles you, revealing the depth of your
wretchedness, its purpose is to exalt and
uplift you. Even though it empties you of
all feeling and detaches you from all natural
pleasures, its purpose is to fill you with
spiritual joy and attach you to the source
of that joy.

St John of the Cross (1542–91), Spain

246 Bitter-sweet

Ah my dear angry Lord,
Since thou dost love, yet strike;
Cast down, yet help afford;
Sure I will do the like.

I will complain, yet praise;
I will bewail, approve:
And all my sour-sweet days
I will lament and love.

George Herbert (1593–1633), England

247 Footprints

You are the sweet kernel of adversity,
    the rescue that sets an ambush
    for all the world's kidnappers.
Your compassion dwells in the cave-
    city of all the world's desperados.
You are to be found within, above;
    but also I can see your footprints
    crisscrossing all the
    world's deserts.

Amicai Weizman (1888–1950), Israel

248 *Patience*

Our real blessings often appear to us in the shapes of pains, losses and disappointments; but let us have patience, and we soon shall see them in their proper figures.

Joseph Addison (1672–1719), England

Do not despair, saying, "My life is gone, and
the Friend has not come." He comes ... and out
of season. He comes not only at dawn.

Jalil al-Din Rumi (1207–73), Persia

The loving gaze

A Sufi master was sitting quietly, when a group of
men came to punish him for wrongs he was accused
of committing. The men rained blows on the Sufi
master, hitting him a thousand times. Yet the Sufi
master remained silent, and no sign of pain
appeared on his face.

After they had finished beating him, the men took
the Sufi master to the court.

The judges asked:
"How did you suffer no pain when you were beaten?"

The Sufi master replied:
"When the men were raining blows on me, my
beloved wife was looking on. Her love made the pain
seem easier. Then I thought that, if the loving gaze
of a human being can ease pain, the loving gaze of
God can eliminate pain altogether."

Nasir al-Din (1201–74), Persia

251 Nature's nourishment

No place of exile is so barren that it can't
abundantly support a man. It's the mind that
creates our wealth and this goes with us into
exile, and in the harshest desert places it
finds enough to nourish the body and revels
in the enjoyment of its own goods.

Seneca (c.4BCE–c.65CE), Rome

252 The solitary traveller

Although they have tightly bound
    my arms and legs,
All over the mountains I hear the
    song of birds,
And the forest is filled
With the perfume of spring flowers.
Who can prevent me from freely
    enjoying these,
Which take from the long journey
A little of its loneliness?

Ho Chi Minh (1890–1969),
from Prison Diary, *Vietnam*

253 *Heart's ease*

Cliffs that rise a thousand feet
    without a break,
Lakes that stretch a hundred miles
    without a wave,
Sands that are white through all the year,
    without a stain,
Pine-tree woods, winter and summer,
    ever green,
Streams that forever flow and flow
    without a pause,
Trees that for twenty thousand years
    your vows have kept,
You have suddenly healed the pain of a
    traveller's heart.

Chang Fang-sheng (4th century), China

the way

255 The ambitious soul

The way is not inconsequential, whether we move forward or backward along it. The place and the way are inside a person. The place is the blissful state of the ambitious soul, the way is the constant change of the ambitious soul.

Søren Kierkegaard (1813–55), Denmark

254 The riddle of the path

You cannot tread the Path before you become the Path yourself.

Zen saying

256 *On solid ground*

The old men used to say: If you see a young person climbing up to heaven by his own will, hold him by the foot, and pull him down to the ground, for it is just not good for him.

From the sayings of the Desert Fathers (5th century), Egypt

257 *Travel easy*

Easy is right.
Begin right and you are easy.
Continue easy and you are right.

Chuang Tzu (d.275BCE), China

To Him who is everywhere,

folk come not by travelling but by loving.

St Augustine of Hippo (354–430), North Africa

Love's wings

The way to heaven is within. Shake the wings of love —
when love's wings have become strong, there is no need
to trouble about a ladder.

Jalil al-Din Rumi (1207–73), Persia

260 Energy and calm

If you can work sincerely and correctly on what is at hand, and do so with energy and calm, not allowing distractions, but keeping your spirit pure, as if you had only borrowed it ... hoping for nothing, fearing nothing, but satisfied with modulating your actions to the way of Nature, and with fearless truth in every word you utter, you will live contentedly. And no one can take that from you.

Marcus Aurelius (121–80), Roman emperor

261 A Socratic prayer

Dear Pan and all other gods of this place, grant that I may become good in my heart. May my external possessions not be at war with what is within. Let me regard the wise man as rich. And let my store of gold be no more than a man of moderation can pick up and carry away.

Socrates (469–399BCE), Athens

262 *To be great, be whole*

To be great, be whole: do not exaggerate or
   exclude anything of what is yours.
Be entire in everything. Put all that you are
   into the least you do.
Be like the full moon, living aloft and
   shining everywhere.

Fernando Pessoa (1888–1935), Portugal

263 *The call*

Come, my Way, my Truth, my Life:
Such a Way, as gives us breath:
Such a Truth, as ends all strife:
Such a Life, as killeth death.

Come, my Light, my Feast, my Strength:
Such a Light, as shows a feast:
Such a Feast, as mends in length:
Such a Strength, as makes his guest.

Come, my Joy, my Love, my Heart:
Such a Joy, as none can move:
Such a Love, as none can part:
Such a Heart, as joys in love.

George Herbert (1593–1633), England

264 *Looking and asking*

Stand at the crossroads, and look,
　　and ask for the ancient paths,
where the good way lies, and walk in it,
　　and find rest for your souls.

Jeremiah *6:16*

265 Paths and deserts

The earth beneath our feet takes many
forms. Some only ride on paths, while
others ride across trackless deserts. Those
who ride on paths are like those who can
see the way to God. Those who ride across
trackless deserts are like those who have
lost the way to God. Yet God reveals
himself within the souls of both; he is
the inner reality of all humankind.

Ibn al-'Arabi (1165–1240), Spain

266 Striving

By attempting the impossible one can
attain the highest level of the possible.

August Strindberg (1849–1912), Sweden

267 Contradictions

Only when you drink from the river of silence shall
    you indeed sing,
and when you have reached the mountain top, then you
    shall begin to climb.
And when the earth shall claim your limbs, then shall
    you truly dance.

Kahlil Gibran (1883–1931), Lebanon

268 How to live

Let the beauty we love be what we do.

Jalil al-Din Rumi (1207–1273), Persia

270 *The way of experience*

Let me use suspense as material for perseverance:
Let me use danger as material for courage:
Let me use reproach as material for long suffering:
Let me use praise as material for humility:
Let me use pleasure as material for temperance:
Let me use pain as material for endurance.

John Baillie (1886–1960), Scotland

269 *Stories*

Maybe there are only three kinds of stories:
The stories we live,
The stories we tell,
And the stories that help our souls
Fly up towards the greater light.

Ben Okri (b.1959), Nigeria

271   *Our life*

The fact that our task is exactly as large as our life makes it infinite.

Franz Kafka (1883–1924), Austria

272 *The motive for worship*

O God! if I worship Thee in fear of Hell, burn
me in Hell; and if I worship Thee
in hope of Paradise, exclude me from Paradise;
but if I worship Thee for
Thine own sake, withold not Thine
Everlasting Beauty!

Rabi'a al-Adawiyya (717–801), Mesopotamia

273 The cloud of unknowing

Lift up your heart to God with humble love; and mean God himself, and not what you get out of him. When you first begin, you find only darkness, and as it were a cloud of unknowing — but still go on longing after him whom you love. For if you are to feel him or to see him in this life, it must always be in this cloud, in this darkness.

Julian of Norwich (c.1342–c.1413), England

274 Flowers of the spirit

We may speak of love and humility as the true flowers of spiritual growth; and they give off a wonderful scent, which benefits all those who come near. The purpose of ecstatic prayer is to enable these flowers to bloom — In ecstatic prayer, without any effort, the Lord raises the soul from the Earth and lifts it to Heaven.

St Teresa of Avila (1515–82), Spain

275 The way of intensity

We are making hay when we should be making
whoopee; we are raising tomatoes when we
should be raising Cain, or Lazarus.

Annie Dillard (b.1945), USA

276 Remembrance

Remembrance of what is good keeps us high
in spirit. Remembrance of what is beautiful
is the salvation of mortal men. Remembrance
of what is dear will be happiness, if it remains
alive. Rememembrance of the One is still the
best thing I know.

Johann Wolfgang von Goethe (1749–1832), Germany

277   *In readiness*

One should be ever booted and spurred and ready to depart.

Michel Eyquem de Montaigne (1533–92), France

278   *Homecoming*

Home is not around the hearth,
    it is within the heart.
Any worthwhile pilgrimage brings us home,
    and so does any distant voyage
      for the sake of love.

Donald Masterson (b.1940), from "Love's Compass", Canada

279   *Offshore*

We do not discover new lands without consenting to
lose sight of the shore for a very long time.

André Gide (1869–1951), France

280 *Exultation ...*

Exultation is the going
Of an inland soul to sea,
Past the houses – past the headlands –
Into deep Eternity –

Bred as we, among the mountains,
Can the sailor understand
The divine intoxication
Of the first league out from land?

Emily Dickinson (1830–86), USA

a world of kinship

281 The acquisition of excellence

Appreciation is a wonderful thing. It makes what
is excellent in others belong to us as well.

Voltaire (1694–1778), France

282 The song of difference

The more we let each voice sing
out with its own true tone,
the richer will be the diversity of
the chant in unison.

Angelus Silesius (1624–77), Poland

283 Gentle strength

When spiders unite, they can tie up a lion.

Ethiopian proverb

284 *Hospitality*

The runaway slave came to my house and stopped
   outside,
I heard his motions crackling the twigs of the
   woodpile,
Through the swung half-door of the kitchen I saw him
   limpsy and weak,
And went where he sat on a log and led him in and
   assured him,
And brought water and filled a tub for his sweated
   body and bruised feet,
And gave him a room that entered from my own, and I
   gave him some coarse clean clothes,
And remember perfectly well his revolving eyes and his
   awkwardness,
And remember putting plasters on the galls of his neck
   and ankles;
He stayed with me a week before he was recuperated
   and passed north.
I had him sit next me at table, my fire-lock leaned in
   the corner.

Walt Whitman (1819–92), from "Song of Myself", USA

285 Entertaining strangers

Let brotherly love continue.
Be not forgetful to entertain strangers: for thereby some have entertained angels unawares.

Hebrews *13:1*

286 Praying and loving

He prayeth well, who loveth well
Both man and bird and beast.

Samuel Taylor Coleridge (1772–1834), England

287 *The heart's new capital*

Gentle souls, walk with me sometimes through
the breath of strangers, which parts like rain,
tremblingly brushes your cheeks, then behind you
with a parting tremble joins together again.

Strong, compassionate ones who reach the plateau
of the heart's new capital, settle here, mark
how your arrows love the bull's-eye and the bow,
how tears extend your eyesight through the dark.

Don't be afraid to suffer. Learn to give back
heaviness to the dead weight of the Earth,
its mountains and seas, nothingness to the black

hole inside the Earth's core. Though all the trees
you planted as children now have the girth
of monsters, still there are spaces ... and the breeze.

after Rainer Maria Rilke (1875–1926), Austria

288 *A perfect chord*

The diversity of the family should be a cause of love
and harmony, as it is in music where many different
notes blend together in the making of a perfect chord.

From the Baha'i Scriptures *(19th century), Persia*

289 *My congregation*

Wherever I am, there in spirit is my congregation also – I
cannot be separated from my people. We may be separated
by space but we are united by love – even if my body dies,
my soul will survive – and my soul will remember my people.

My congregation is my family; its members are my parents,
my brothers and sisters, and my children. They are dearer to
me than light – their love is weaving for me a crown that I
shall wear for all eternity.

St John Chrysostom (c.345–c.407), Turkey

Belonging

We owe our respect to a collectivity of whatever kind — country, family or any other — not for itself, but because it is food for a certain number of human souls.

Simone Weil (1909–49), France

One soul

I believe in the absolute oneness of God and therefore also of humanity. What though we have many bodies? We have but one soul.

Mahatma Gandhi (1869–1948), India

292 Bread and water

Our bread and water are of one table:

the progeny of Adam are as a single soul.

Muhammad Iqbal (1877–1958), India

a world of harmony

293 *Love the whole tree*

Love not the shapely branch,
Nor place its image alone in your heart.
It dies away.

Love the whole tree;
Then you will love the shapely branch,
The tender and withered leaf,
The shy bud and the full-blown flower,
The falling petal and the dancing night,
The splendid shadow of full love.

Ah, love Life in its fullness.
It knows no decay.

Jiddu Krishnamurti (1895–1986), India

295 The humble worm

Lands that are subject to frequent
inundations are always poor; and
probably the reason may be
because the worms are drowned.
The most insignificant insects
and reptiles are of much more
consequence, and have much
more influence in the economy
of nature, than the incurious are
aware of; and are mighty in their
effect, from their minuteness,
which renders them less an object
of attention; and from their
numbers and fecundity. Earth-
worms, though in appearance
a small and despicable link in the
chain of nature, yet, if lost, would
make a lamentable chasm.

Gilbert White (1720–93), England

294 Nothing is useless

Among all the things that the Holy
One, blessed be He, created in His
Universe, He created nothing that
is useless. He created the snail as
a cure for scab, the fly as a cure
for the sting of the wasp, the gnat
as a cure for the bite of the serpent,
the serpent as a cure for a sore, and
the spider as a cure for the sting
of a scorpion.

From the Talmud *(6th century)*

296 Sun and stars

The sun and stars that float in the open air ... the
    appleshaped Earth and we upon it ... surely the drift
    of them is something grand;
I do not know what it is except that it is grand, and that it is
    happiness ...

Walt Whitman (1819–92), from "Song of Myself", USA

297 To a young athlete

Thing of a day! Such is man: a shadow in a dream.
Yet when god-given splendour visits him,
a bright radiance plays over him, and then how sweet is life.

Pindar (552–442BCE), Greece

298 The magic word

A song slumbers in all things
that lie dreaming on and on
and the world prepares to sing,
if you hit upon the magic word.

Joseph Freiherr von Eichendorff
(1788–1857), Germany

299 *Heaven on Earth*

Now that it is night,
you fetch in the washing
from outer space,

from the frozen garden
filmed like a kidney,
with a ghost in your mouth,

and everything you hold,
two floating shirts, a sheet,
ignores the law of gravity.

Only this morning,
the wren at her millinery,
making a baby's soft bonnet,

as we stopped by the spring,
watching the water
well up in the grass,

as if the world were teething.
It was heaven on earth
and it was only the morning.

Craig Raine (b.1944), England

Morning and evening

In the house made of dawn.
In the story made of dawn.
On the trail of dawn.
O, Talking God.
His feet, my feet, restore.
His limbs, my limbs, restore.
His body, my body, restore.
His voice, my voice, restore.
His plumes, my plumes, restore.
With beauty below him, with beauty below me.
With beauty around him, with beauty around me.
With pollen beautiful in his voice,
With pollen beautiful in my voice.
It is finished in beauty.
It is finished in beauty.
In the house of evening light.
From the story made of evening light.
On the trail of evening light.

Native American song, USA

301 *Holy Thursday*

'Twas on a Holy Thursday, their innocent faces clean,
The children walking two and two, in red and blue and green,
Grey-headed beadles walked before, with wands as white as snow,
Till into the high dome of Paul's they like Thames' waters flow.

O what a multitude they seemed, these flowers of London town!
Seated in companies they sit with radiance all their own.
The hum of multitudes was there, but multitudes of lambs,
Thousands of little boys and girls raising their innocent hands.

Now like a mighty wind they raise to heaven the voice of song,
Or like harmonious thunderings the seats of heaven among.
Beneath them sit the aged men, wise guardians of the poor;
Then cherish pity, lest you drive an angel from your door.

William Blake (1757–1827), England

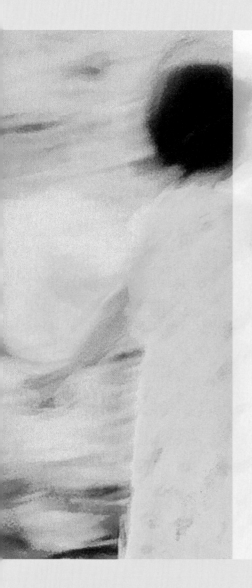

302 *Meeting the sun*

The smoke of my own breath,
Echoes, ripples, buzzed whispers, love-root, silk-thread,
    crotch and vine,
My respiration and inspiration, the beating of my heart,
    the passing of blood and air through my lungs,
The sniff of green leaves and dry leaves, and of the shore
    and dark-colored sea-rocks, and of hay in the barn,
The sound of the belched words of my voice loosed to the
    eddies of the wind,
A few light kisses, a few embraces, a reaching around
    of arms,
The play of shine and shade on the trees as the supple
    boughs wag,
The delight alone or in the rush of the streets, or along
    the fields and hillsides,
The feeling of health, the full-noon trill, the song of me
    rising from bed and meeting the sun.

Walt Whitman (1819–92), from "Song of Myself", USA

The birthright

We who were born
In country places,
Far from cities
And shifting faces,
We have a birthright
No man can sell,
And a secret joy
No man can tell.

For we are kindred
To lordly things,
The wild duck's flight
And the white owl's wings;
To pike and salmon,
To bull and horse,
The curlew's cry
And the smell of gorse.

Pride of trees,
Swiftness of streams,
Magic of frost
Have shaped our dreams:
No baser vision
Their spirit fills
Who walk by right
On the naked hills.

Eiluned Lewis (1900–1979), Wales

304 *The sea-cliff*

Here come soaring
White gulls
Leisurely wheeling
In air over islands,
Sea pinks and salt grass,
Gannet and eider,
Curlew and cormorant
Each a differing
Pattern of ecstasy
Recurring at nodes
In an on-flowing current,
The perpetual species,
Repeated, renewed
By the will of joy
In eggs lodged safe
On perilous ledges.

Kathleen Raine (b.1908), from
"The Moment", England

305 *Tall nettles*

Tall nettles cover up, as they have done
These many springs, the rusty harrow,
    the plough
Long worn out, and the roller made of stone:
Only the elm butt tops the nettles now.

This corner of the farmyard I like most:
As well as any bloom upon a flower
I like the dust on the nettles, never lost
Except to prove the sweetness of a shower.

Edward Thomas (1878–1917), England

306 *Cosmic love*

... love the universe as one's city, one's
native country, the beloved fatherland of
every soul.

Simone Weil (1909–43), France

307 *The sacred earth*

Every part of this earth is sacred to my people.
Every shining pine needle, every sandy shore, every mist
in the dark wood, every clearing and humming insect
is holy in the memory and experience of my people ...
We are part of the earth and it is part of us.

*Chief Seathl (19th century), from "Chief Seathl's
Testament", USA*

308 *Love is my king*

Love is and was my Lord and King,
    And in his presence I attend
    To hear the tidings of my friend,
Which every hour his couriers bring.

Love is and was my King and Lord,
    And will be, though as yet I keep
    Within his court on earth, and sleep
Encompassed by his faithful guard,

And hear at times a sentinel
    Who moves about from place to place,
    And whispers to the worlds of space,
In the deep night, that all is well.

Alfred, Lord Tennyson (1809–92),
from "In Memoriam", England

a world of peace

309   *Harvesting*

     Let us aim to harvest peace.
     Let us exhaust ourselves in ploughing
          the stony ground.

     Modern prayer from Turkey

310   *The hall of peace*

     If anyone throws a stone,
          may it be only to mark the limits
          of the new foundations –

     a great Hall of Peace in which we will all
          give thanks to the Merciful Lord.

     Modern prayer from Sri Lanka

311 Grass in the wind

You who govern public affairs,
what need have you to employ
punishments? Love virtue, and the
people will be virtuous. The virtues
of a superior man are like the wind;
the virtues of a common man are
like the grass; the grass, when
the wind passes over it, bends.

Henry David Thoreau (1817–62), USA

312 The harmonious kingdom

First there must be order and harmony within
your own mind. Then this order will spread
to your family, then to the community, and
finally to your entire kingdom. Only then can
you have peace and harmony.

Confucius (551–479BCE), China

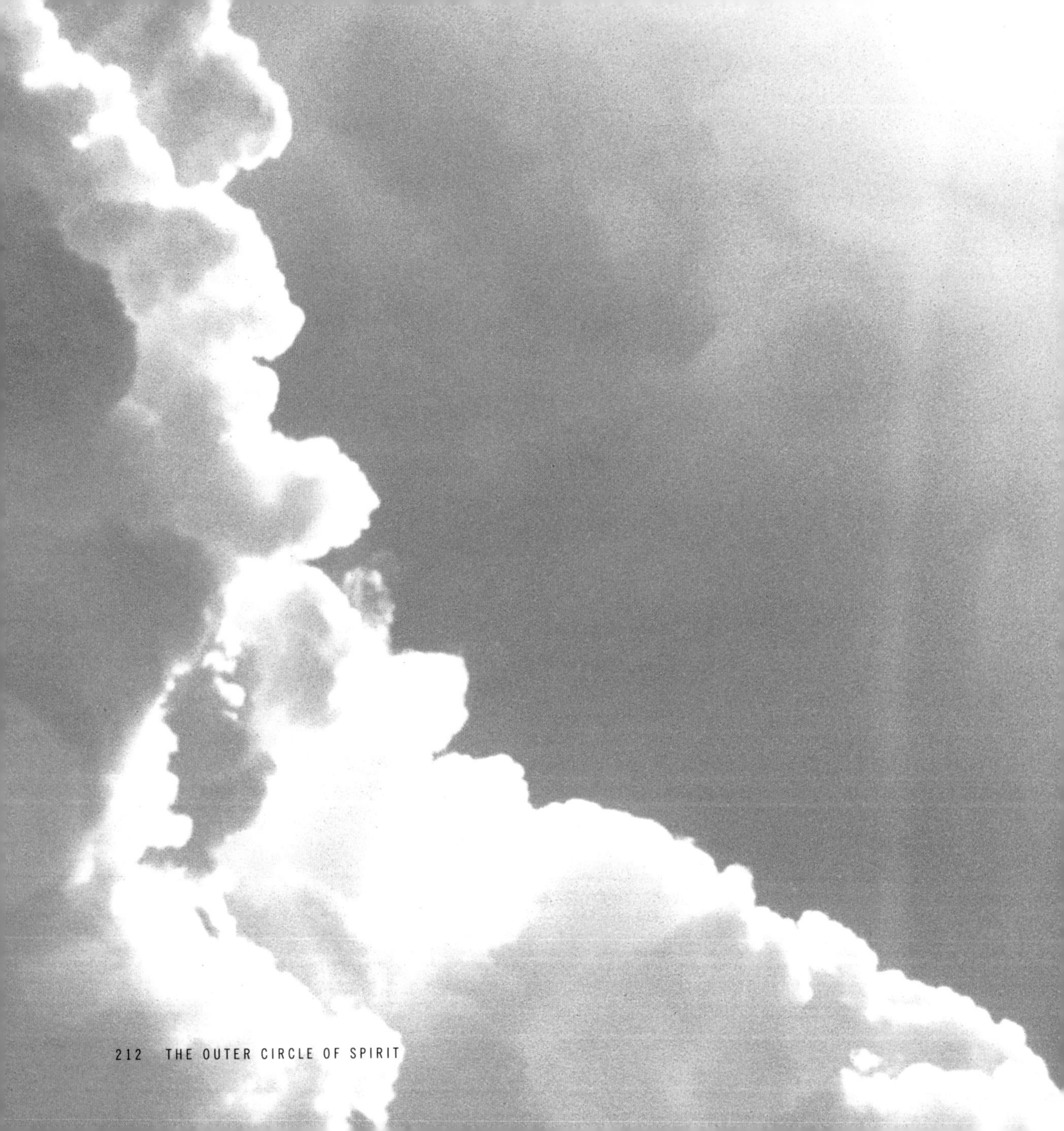

313 *Divine sunlight*

Abiding in Her magnificent shrine,
She shines Her protecting rays far
to the lands of the four corners,
Her radiant light bringing peace
everywhere under the heavens.

Inscription at the Ise Shrine, Japan (referring to the sun goddess, Amaterasu)

the one

314   *God's name*

And I say to mankind, Be not curious about God,
For I who am curious about each am not curious about God.
(No array of terms can say how much I am at peace about
    God and about death.)

I hear and behold God in every object, yet understand God
    not in the least,
Nor do I understand who there can be more wonderful than
    myself.
Why should I wish to see God better than this day?
I see something of God each hour of the twenty-four, and
    each moment then,
In the faces of men and women I see God, and in my own
    face in the glass,
I find letters from God dropped in the street, and every one
    is signed by God's name,
And I leave them where they are, for I know that
    wheresoever I go,
Others will punctually come for ever and ever.

Walt Whitman (1819–92), from "Song of Myself", USA

315   *Who has seen the wind?*

Who has seen the wind?
Neither I nor you:
But when the leaves hang trembling
The wind is passing through.

Who has seen the wind?
Neither you nor I:
But when the trees bow down their heads
The wind is passing by.

Christina Rossetti (1830–94), England

316   *Omnipresence*

Called or not called, God is
always there.

Carl Jung (1875–1961), Switzerland

317 A sheltering heart

I asked for Peace – My sins arose,
And bound me close,
I could not find release.

I asked for Truth – My doubts came in,
And with their din
They wearied all my youth.

I asked for Love – My lovers failed,
And griefs assailed
Around, beneath, above.

I asked for Thee – And Thou didst come
To take me home
Within Thy heart to be.

D.M. Dolben (1848–67), England

318 *Light in all corners*

God's wisdom must be regarded as the unique
source of all light upon Earth, even such feeble
lights as those which illumine the things of the
world.

Simone Weil (1909–43), France

319 *The world in my hand*

In his love he clothes us, enfolds and embraces us; that
tender love completely surrounds us, never to leave us ...
he showed me more, a little thing, the size of a hazelnut
on the palm of my hand, round like a ball. I looked at it
thoughtfully and wondered, "What is this?" And the answer
came, "It is all that is made. ... It exists, both now and for
ever, because God loves it."

Julian of Norwich (c.1342–c.1413), England

320 God's goodness

"In you alone do I have all." Such
words are dear indeed unto the soul,
and very close to the will and goodness
of God. For he himself is eternity,
and has made us for himself alone,
has restored us by his blessed passion
and keeps us in his blessed love. And
all because he is goodness.

Julian of Norwich (c.1342–c.1413), England

321 The all-seeing

However wild
He may be,
God can see,
God can save.

Anonymous (c.1370), from Sir Gawain and the
Green Knight, *England*

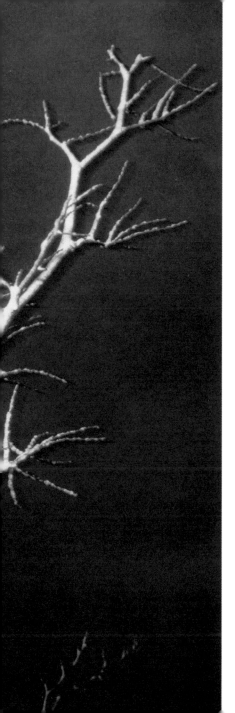

The lord of opposites

God is in the water of the lake; he is also in the cracked bed of the lake when the lake has dried up.

God is in the abundant harvest; he is also in the famine that occurs when the harvest fails.

God is in the lightning; he is also in the darkness when the lightning has faded.

Mansur al-Hallaj (858–922), Persia

Awaken to the changeless

All is change in the world of the senses,

but changeless is the supreme Lord of Love.

Meditate on him, be absorbed in him,

wake up from this dream of separateness.

From the Svetasvatara Upanishad *(600–300BCE), India*

When your mind, that may be wavering in the contradictions of many scriptures, shall rest unshaken in divine contemplation, then the goal of union is yours.

From the Bhagavad Gita *(1st–2nd century), India*

325 $\mathcal{O}m$

OM is the supreme symbol of the Lord.
OM is the whole. OM affirms; OM signals
the chanting of the hymns from the Vedas.
The priest begins with OM; spiritual teachers
and their students begin with OM.
The student who is established in OM
becomes united with the Lord of Love.

From the Taittiriya Upanishad *(600–300BCE), India*

326 $\mathcal{T}he\ self\ and\ the\ lord\ of\ love$

Like oil in sesame seeds, like butter
in cream, like water in springs, like fire
in firesticks, so dwells the Lord of Love,
the Self, in the very depths of consciousness.
Realize him through truth and meditation.

From the Svetashvatara Upanishad *(600–300BCE), India*

The deepest perception

The more perfect and pure the powers of the soul
are, the more perfectly and comprehensively they
can receive the object of their perception, embracing
and experiencing a greater bliss, and the more they
become one with that which they percieve, to such
a degree indeed that the highest power of the soul,
which is free of all things and which has nothing in
common with anything else at all, perceives nothing
less than God himself in the breadth and fullness
of his being.

Meister Eckhart (1260–1327), Germany

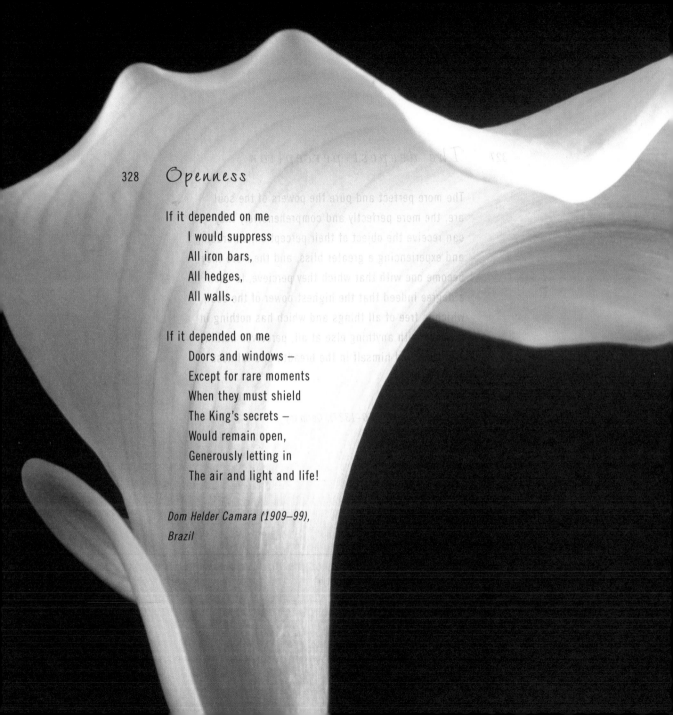

Openness

If it depended on me
    I would suppress
    All iron bars,
    All hedges,
    All walls.

If it depended on me
    Doors and windows —
    Except for rare moments
    When they must shield
    The King's secrets —
    Would remain open,
    Generously letting in
    The air and light and life!

Dom Helder Camara (1909–99),
Brazil

329　*Love's fragrance*

Make us, O Lord, flourish like pure, white lilies
in the court of your house, giving forth the
sweet fragrance of your love to all who pass.

Mozarabic Sacramentary (3rd century), Spain

330　*The heart's revelation*

I saw my Lord with the eye of my heart, and
I said: "Who art Thou?"
He said: "Thou."

Mansur al-Hallaj (858–922), Persia

331　*One place*

Whether I fly with angels, fall with dust,
　Thy hands made both, and I am there:
Thy power and love, my love and trust,
　Make one place everywhere.

George Herbert (1593–1633), from "The Temper", England

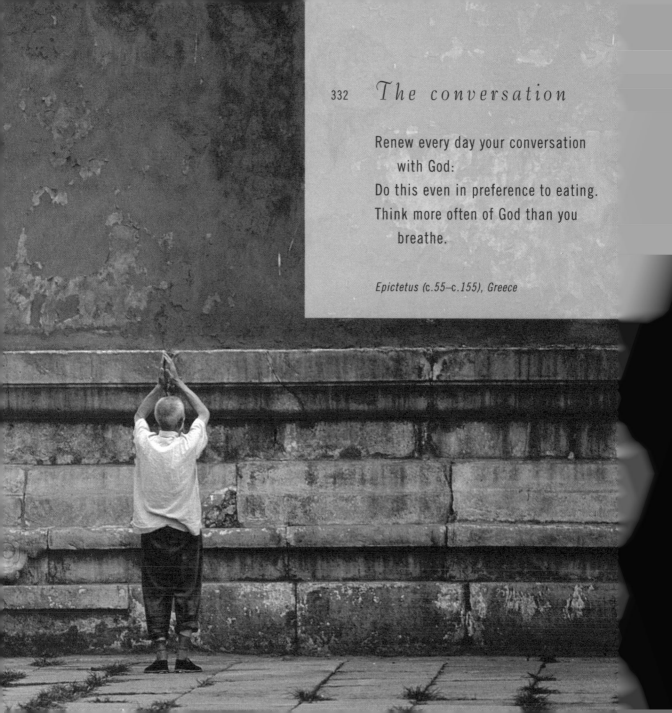

332 *The conversation*

Renew every day your conversation
with God:
Do this even in preference to eating.
Think more often of God than you
breathe.

Epictetus (c.55–c.155), Greece

333 Adam's song

I, I have strayed far from Your Keep
But I will return to Your Heart.

I, I have strayed far from Your Name
But I will return to Your Breath.

I, I have strayed far from Your Love
But I will return to Your Peace.

Jay Ramsay (b.1946), England

334 Infinite love

At each beat of my heart I want, O my Beloved, to
renew my offering to you an infinite number of
times, until the shadows have disappeared and I
can tell you of my love face to face in eternity.

St Thérèse of Lisieux (1873–97), France

near and far horizons

335 *Immortality*

My eyes want to flow into each other
like two neighbouring lakes.

To tell each other
everything they've seen.

My blood has many relatives.
They never visit.

But when they die,
my blood will inherit.

Yehuda Amichai (1924–2000), Israel

336 *Between two nothings*

Invisible before birth are all beings and after death invisible again.
They are seen between two unseens. Why in this truth find sorrow?

From the Bhagavad Gita *(1st–2nd century), India*

337   The last horizon

As we climbed up the mountain and came
to where I thought the horizon would be,
it had disappeared – another horizon was
waiting further on. I was disappointed,
but also excited in an unfamiliar way.
Each new level had revealed a new world.
Against this perspective, death can be
understood as the final horizon. Beyond
there, the deepest well of your identity
awaits you. In that well, you will behold
the beauty and light of your eternal face.

John O'Donohue (b.1956), Ireland

338 *Resurrection in time*

I feel, looking back upon the past, that – since I left
school I have had – like many, I suspect, of my War
generation contemporaries – two quite separate lives –
The fact that, within ten years, I lost one world and
after a time rose again, as it were, from spiritual death to
find another, seems to me one of the strongest arguments
against suicide that life can provide – resurrection is
possible within our limited span of earthly time.

Vera Brittain (1894–1970), England

339 *The span of life*

Is there not a certain satisfaction in the fact that natural
limits are set to the life of the individual, so that at the
conclusion it may appear as a work of art?

Albert Einstein (1879–1955), Germany

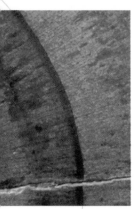

340   *The beetle's egg*

Every one has heard the story which has gone the
rounds of New England, of a strong and beautiful
bug which came out of the dry leaf of an old table of
apple-tree wood, which had stood in a farmer's
kitchen for sixty years, first in Connecticut, and
afterward in Massachusetts – from an egg deposited
in the living tree many years earlier still, as
appeared by counting the annual layers beyond it;
which was heard gnawing out for several weeks,
hatched perchance by the heat of an urn. Who does
not feel his faith in a resurrection and immortality
strengthened by hearing of this?

Henry David Thoreau (1817–62), USA

341   *Facing mortality*

When you die, it will be not because you are sick,
but because you were alive.

Seneca (c.4BCE–c.65CE), Rome

The unknown

Life is a great surprise. I do not see why
death should not be an even greater one.

Vladimir Nabokov (1899–1977), USA

Dying is a wild night
and a new road.

Emily Dickinson (1830–86), USA

344 Soul and body

The spirit looks upon the dust
That fastened it so long
With indignation,
As a Bird
Defrauded of its song.

Emily Dickinson (1830–86), USA

345 Impossibility

Thou in me and I in thee. Death! what is
death? There is no death: *in thee* it is
impossible, absurd.

Mark Rutherford (1829–1913), England

346 *The parting*

When the parting suddenly flings wide forever
The unknown distance, in a little while,
I'll remember everything by name, by the quiver
Of their wise and bashful smile.

I shall put my dead face on with a silence free
Of joy and of pain evermore,
And dawn will trail like a child after me
To play with shells on the shore.

Yocheved Bat-Miriam (1901–79), born in Russia,
settled in Palestine

347 *The triumph of life*

And death shall have no dominion.
Dead men naked they shall be one
With the man in the wind and the west moon;
When their bones are picked clean and the clean bones gone,
They shall have stars at elbow and foot;
Though they go mad they shall be sane,
Though they sink through the sea they shall rise again;
Though lovers be lost love shall not;
And death shall have no dominion.

Dylan Thomas (1914–53), from "And death shall have no dominion", Wales

348 *Leavetaking*

My delight in death
exceeds the pleasure of a merchant
who makes a vast fortune,
or a victorious war god,
or a sage in total trance.
Like a traveller taking to the road,
I will leave this world and return home ...
My life is over and my karma is done with ...
I am approaching the ground of primal perfection.

Longchenpa (1308–63), Tibet

349 When the time comes

When the time comes, I will know that death is a homecoming,
  not a wrench that leaves a bruise on my spirit.

Death is not the shadow but the light beyond the shadow.

My spirit will return to its resting place
  in a long, slow glide toward peace.

Modern meditation from Orkney, Scotland

350 The flight of the soul

Pure, goodly soul, how long will you journey on?
You are the King's falcon. Fly back toward the
Emperor's whistle!

Jalil al-Din Rumi (1207–73), Persia

351 The empty chamber

Go sweep the chamber of your heart. Make it ready to be the dwelling-place of the Beloved. When you depart, He will enter it. In you, empty of yourself, He will display all his beauty.

Shabistari (b.1936), Iran

352 $\mathcal{D}awn$

O Night and Dark,
O huddled sullen clouds,
Light enters in the sky
Whitens.
Christ comes! Depart! Depart!

The mist sheers apart,
Cleft by the sun's spear.
Colour comes back to things
From his bright face.

Prudentius (c.348–c.410), from "At a beautiful dawn,
after bad weather", Spain

353 The eternal now

Not with thoughts of your mind, but in the believing
sweetness of your heart, you snap the link and open the
golden door and disappear into the bright room, the
everlasting ecstasy, eternal Now.

Jack Kerouac (1923–69), USA

354 *She*

I think the dead are tender. Shall we kiss? —
My lady laughs, delighting in what is.
If she but sighs, a bird puts out its tongue.
She makes space lonely with a lovely song.
She lilts a low soft language, and I hear
Down long sea-chambers of the inner ear.

We sing together; we sing mouth to mouth.
The garden is a river flowing south.
She cries out loud the soul's own secret joy;
She dances, and the ground bears her away.
She knows the speech of light, and makes it plain
A lively thing can come to life again.

I feel her presence in the common day,
In that slow walk that widens every eye.
She moves as water moves, and comes to me,
Stayed by what was, and pulled by what would be.

Theodore Roethke (1908–63), USA

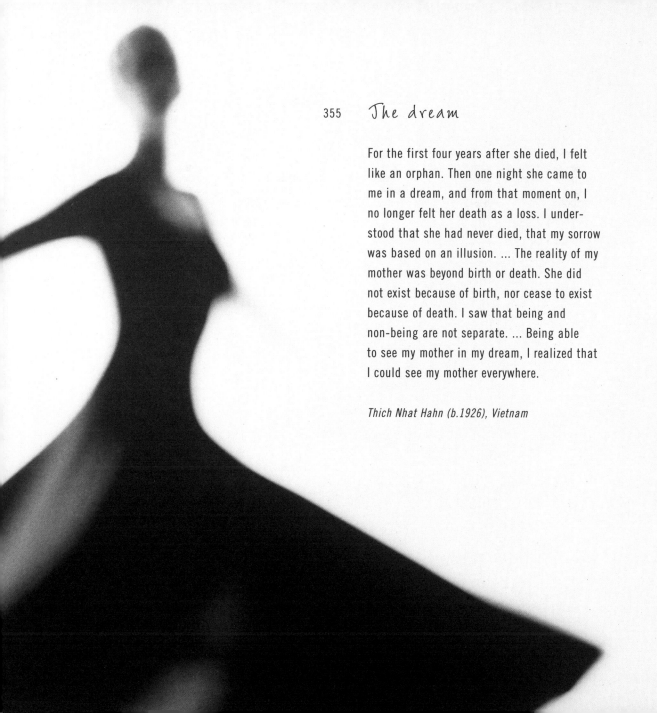

The dream

For the first four years after she died, I felt
like an orphan. Then one night she came to
me in a dream, and from that moment on, I
no longer felt her death as a loss. I understood that she had never died, that my sorrow
was based on an illusion. ... The reality of my
mother was beyond birth or death. She did
not exist because of birth, nor cease to exist
because of death. I saw that being and
non-being are not separate. ... Being able
to see my mother in my dream, I realized that
I could see my mother everywhere.

Thich Nhat Hahn (b.1926), Vietnam

356   *The imprisoned soul*

At the last, tenderly,
From the walls of the powerful, fortressed house,
From the clasp of the knitted locks – from the keep
    of the well-closed doors,
Let me be wafted.

Let me glide noiselessly forth;
With the key of softness unlock the locks –
    with a whisper
Set ope the doors, O soul!

Walt Whitman (1819–92), USA

357   *The first stage*

The grave is the first stage of the journey
into eternity.

Muhammad (570–632)

358 *Hidden treasure*

The kingdom of heaven is like treasure hidden in a field, which someone found and hid; then in his joy he goes and sells all that he has and buys that field.

Matthew *13:44*

359 *A place to rest*

Thou art the true peace of the heart, Thou art its only rest; out of Thee all things are full of trouble and difficulty. In this peace, that is, in Thee, the one sovereign eternal Good, I will sleep and take my rest. Amen.

Thomas à Kempis (1380–1471), Germany

eternity

360   *The anthem of boundless spirit*

Behold, I have reached the peak of the mountain and
my spirit has taken flight in the heavens of freedom
and liberation. I have gone far, far away, O children of
my mother; the hills beyond the mists are now hidden
from my view, the last traces of the valleys have been
flooded by the ocean of serenity, and the paths and
trails have been erased by the hand of oblivion. The
roar of ocean waves has faded. I no longer hear
anything but the anthem of eternity, which
harmonizes with the spirit.

Kahlil Gibran (1883–1931), Lebanon

361   *Mist and sky*

The purity men love is like the mists which envelop
the earth, and not like the azure ether beyond.

Henry David Thoreau (1817–62), USA

362 Dissolution

We,
Like parted drops of rain
Swelling till they melt and run,
Shall be all absorbed
Again –

Melting,
Flowing into one.

Christopher Pearse Cranch (1813–92), USA

363 Time's place

Time of its own power cooks all beings within
itself. No-one, however, knows that in which
Time itself is being cooked.

From the Mahabharata *(6th century BCE), India*

Legacy

Nothing that is can dissolve into nothingness!

In all that lives the Eternal Force works on:

remain, rejoicing, in Being! Being is eternal;

for laws preserve the living treasures with

which the universe has adorned itself.

Johann Wolfgang von Goethe (1749–1832), Germany

To every one of us there must come a time when the whole universe will be found to have been a dream, when we find the soul is infinitely better than its surroundings. It is only a question of time, and time is nothing in the infinite.

Shirdi Sai Baba (1856–1918), India

index of first lines

index of authors and sources

acknowledgments

Acknowledgments have been listed by quotation number.

3 from THE RUBAIYAT by Jalil al-Din Rumi, translated by Azima Medita Kolin and Maryam Mafi, translation copyright © Maryam Mafi and Azima Medita Kolin, 1999 (Thorsons, an imprint of HarperCollins); **4, 24, 219, 240** from COLLECTED POEMS OF WALLACE STEVENS by Wallace Stevens, copyright © 1954 by Wallace Stevens and renewed 1982 by Holly Stevens (Faber & Faber, 1955). Reprinted by kind permission of the publishers and Alfred A. Knopf, a division of Random House, Inc., USA; **5, 28, 327** from SELECTED WRITINGS by Meister Eckhart, translated by Oliver Davies, copyright © Oliver Davies, 1994 (Penguin Classics); **10, 156, 353** from THE SCRIPTURE OF THE GOLDEN ETERNITY by Jack Kerouac (City Lights, 1994); **11, 43, 78, 105, 111, 152** from BUDDHA'S LITTLE INSTRUCTION BOOK by Jack Kornfield (Rider, 1996). Reprinted by kind permission of the Random House Group Ltd, UK, and Random House Inc., USA; **12, 55, 276, 364** from GOETHE: SELECTED VERSE, translated by David Luke, copyright © David Luke, 1964 (Penguin Classics); **14, 37, 42, 49, 192, 324** from THE BHAGAVAD GITA, translated by Juan Mascaro, copyright © Juan Mascaro, 1962 (Penguin Classics). Reprinted by kind permission of the publishers; **15, 38, 45, 260** from THE SPIRITUAL TEACHINGS OF MARCUS AURELIUS by Mark Forstater (Hodder Mobius, 2001). Reprinted by kind permission of Hodder and Stoughton Ltd, London, and HarperCollins, New York; **16, 251** from THE SPIRITUAL TEACHINGS OF SENECA by Mark Forstater and Victoria Rodin (Hodder Mobius, 2001). Reprinted by kind permission of Hodder and Stoughton Ltd, London, and Penguin Putnam, New York; **18** from LIFE SENTENCE: SELECTED POEMS by Nina Cassian, translated by Eva Feiler and Nina Cassian, edited by William Jay Smith (Anvil Press, 1990). Reprinted by kind permission of the publishers; **21** from the TAO TE CHING by Lao Tzu, translated by Lombardo and Addiss (Hackett Publishing Company Inc., 1993). Reprinted by kind permission of the publishers; **26** from A GOLDEN TREASURY OF CHINESE POETRY, edited by John Deeney, translated by John Turner (Renditions Books, 1997). Reprinted by kind permission of the publishers; **30, 92, 304** from COLLECTED POEMS by Kathleen Raine (Golgonooza Press, 2000). Reprinted by kind permission of the publishers; **33, 41, 47, 54, 83, 90, 91, 99, 101, 160, 165, 171, 172, 184, 185, 196, 197, 213, 220, 225, 228, 247, 278, 309, 310** translations copyright © Duncan Baird Publishers, London, 2002; **44, 119** from MAGNIFICENT ONE: SELECTIONS FROM RUMI'S DIVAN-I KEBIR by Jalil al-Din Rumi, translated by Nevit Oguz Ergin (Larson Publications, 1993); **46, 218** from BREATHING TRUTH: RUMI QUOTATIONS by Muriel Maufroy (Blue Dolphin Publishing, 1997); **48, 149, 154** from THE WISDOM OF THE TIBETAN LAMAS by Shantideva, copyright © Timothy Freke (Godsfield Press, 1999). Reprinted by kind permission of David & Charles Ltd, London; **50** from THE KORAN INTERPRETED by A. J. Arberry, copyright © A.J. Arberry, 1942. Reprinted by kind permission of HarperCollins Publishers Ltd; **63** from INTRODUCING BUDDHA, translation copyright © Jane Hope (Icon Books Ltd, 1999); **68, 355** from THE HEART OF THE BUDDHA'S TEACHING by Thich Nhat Hanh (Parallax Press, 1998 and paperback by Broadway Books, 1999). Reprinted by kind permission of Parallax Press; **69, 275** from PILGRIM AT TINKER CREEK by Annie Dillard (Harper Collins Perennial, 1998). Reprinted by kind permission of the publishers; **71** from THE HAW LANTERN by Seamus Heaney (Faber & Faber, 1987). Reprinted by kind permission of the publishers and Farrar, Straus & Giroux, New York; **74, 109** from THE DIARY OF A YOUNG GIRL by Anne Frank, translated by Susan Massotty and Euan Cameron, edited by Otto H. Frank and Miriam Pressler (Penguin Books, 2000); **81** from LE PARTI PRIS DES CHOSES by Francis Ponge, edited and translated by Margaret Guiton (Editions Gallimard, 1942). Reprinted by kind permission of Red Dust, New York, and Wake Forest University Press, New York; **82** from THE SELECTED POEMS OF TOMAS TRANSTRÖMER, translated by Robin Fulton (Bloodaxe Books, 1997). Reprinted by kind permission of the publishers; **87** from THE SPIRIT LEVEL by Seamus Heaney (Faber & Faber, 1996). Reprinted by kind permission of the publishers and Farrar, Straus & Giroux, New York; **90** from WILD WAYS: ZEN POEMS OF IKKYU, translated by John Stevens, copyright © 1995. Reprinted by kind permission of Shambhala Publications, Inc., Boston, www.shambhala.com; **95, 125, 256** from DESERT WISDOM: SAYINGS FROM THE DESERT FATHERS by Henri J. M. Nonwen and Yushi Nomura, copyright © 1982, 2001 (Orbis Books, New York). Reprinted by kind permission of the publishers; **104, 140** from COLLECTED POEMS: 1945–1990 by R.S. Thomas (Orion Paperbacks, 2000). Reprinted by kind permission of the publishers; **121, 287** from SONNETS TO ORPHEUS (II, vi, and I,iv), adaptation copyright © Robert Saxton, 2002; **122** translated from Gujarati by Sitanshu Yashashchandra, from THE OXFORD ANTHOLOGY OF MODERN INDIAN POETRY (Oxford University Press, 1997); **123, 333** from KINGDOM OF THE EDGE: POEMS FOR THE SPIRIT by Jay Ramsay (Element Books Ltd, 1999). Reprinted by kind permission of Chrysalis Books Plc, UK; **131** from BURNING GIRAFFES: MODERN AND CONTEMPORARY JAPANESE POETRY, translated by James Hirkup (University of Salzburg Press, 1996); **134** from COLLECTED POEMS: 1909–1939, VOLUME 1 by William Carlos Williams, copyright © New Directions Corp., 1938 (Carcanet Press, 2000). Reprinted by kind permission of New Directions Publishing Corp., New York, and Carcanet Press Ltd, Manchester; **135, 167, 267** from THE VISION: REFLECTIONS ON THE WAY OF THE SOUL by Kahlil Gibran, translated by Juan R. I. Cole translation copyright © Juan R.I. Cole, 1997 (Arkana); **136, 138, 143, 194, 217, 264, 285, 358** The Scripture quotations contained herein are from the New Revised Standard Version Bible, copyright © 1989 by the Division of Christian Education of the National Council of the Churches of Christ in the USA, and are used by permission. All rights reserved; **137** from ANOTHER DAY: PRAYERS OF THE HUMAN FAMILY, compiled and edited by John Carden, copyright © SPCK, London (SPCK, 1986). Reprinted by kind permission of the publishers; **145, 298** translation copyright © Hanne Bewernick, 2002; **168, 173** from RUMI: DAYLIGHT, translated by Camille and Kabir Helminski, copyright © Camille and Kabir Helminski, 1994 (Shambhala). Reprinted by kind permission of Shambhala Publications, Inc., Boston, www.shambhala.com; **169** from COLLECTED POEMS by Elizabeth Jennings, copyright © Elizabeth Jennings (Carcanet Press Ltd, 1987). Reprinted by kind permission of the publishers; **180, 229, 235, 239** from COLLECTED POEMS by Anne Ridler (Carcanet Press Ltd, 1994). Reprinted by kind permission of the publishers; **183** from SELECTED POEMS by Michael Longley (Jonathan Cape, 1998). Reprinted by kind permission of Jonathan Cape, a division of the Random House Group Ltd, London; **186, 207, 215, 360** from THE PROPHET by Kahlil Gibran, copyright © 1923 by Kahlil Gibran and renewed 1951 by Administrators C. T. A. of Kahlil Gibran Estate and Mary G. Gibran (Heinemann, 1993). Reproduced by kind permission of Alfred A. Knopf, a division of Random House, Inc., USA, and Gibran National Committee, P.O. Box 116-5375, Beirut, Lebanon; **195** from NORTH by Seamus Heaney (Faber & Faber, 1996). Reprinted by kind permission of the publishers and Farrar, Straus & Giroux, New York; **204** from THE CHINE by Mimi Khalvati (Carcanet Press Ltd, 2002). Reprinted by kind permission of the publishers; **205** from THE SOVEREIGNTY OF GOOD by Iris Murdoch, copyright © 1971 Iris Murdoch (Routledge, imprint of Taylor and Francis Group). Reprinted by kind permission of the publishers; **210** from COMPLETE POEMS 1904–1962, by E.E. Cummings, edited by George J. Firmage, copyright © 1991 by the Trustees for the E.E. Cummings Trust and George James Firmage (Liveright, 1994). Reprinted by kind permission of W. W. Norton & Company, London; **211** from the "Sian Bhuddha" in THE LITTLE BOOK OF CELTIC BLESSINGS, compiled by Caitlin Matthews, copyright © Caitlin Matthews, 1994 (Element Books Ltd). Reprinted by kind permission of HarperCollins Publishers Ltd, London; **212** from THE INK DARK MOON by Jane Hirschfield and Mariko Aratani, copyright © Jane Hirschfield and Mariko Aratani, 1990 (Vintage Classics, 1990). Reprinted by kind permission of Vintage Books, a division of Random House, Inc., New York; **222** from THE DIVINE COMEDY by Dante Alighieri, translated by John D. Sinclair © 1939 (Oxford University Press); **230, 346** from HEBREW LOVE POEMS, edited by David C. Gross, copyright © David C. Gross (Hippocrene Books, 1995). Reprinted by kind permission of the publishers; **232** from SELECTED POEMS by Pauline Stainer (Bloodaxe Books). Reprinted by kind permission of the publishers; **236** from AN ANTHOLOGY OF VIETNAMESE POEMS, edited and translated by Huynsh Sash Thong (Yale University Press, 1996); **237** copyright © Derek Mahon. Reprinted by kind permission of the Gallery Press, County Meath, Ireland; **241** from THE EYES by Antonio Machado, adaptation by Don Paterson (Faber & Faber, 1999). Reprinted by kind permission of the publishers; **243** from THE POCKET RUMI READER, copyright © Kabir Helminski, 2001 (Shambhala). Reprinted by kind permission of Shambhala Publications, Inc., Boston, www.shambhala.com; **261** from PLATO: SYMPOSIUM and PHAEDERUS, translated by Tom Griffith, translation copyright © Tom Griffith, 1986 (Everyman's Library). Reprinted by kind permission of the author; **269** from BIRDS OF HEAVEN by Ben Okri, copyright © Ben Okri (Phoenix House and

Orion). Reprinted by kind permission of David Godwin Associates, London; **270** from A DIARY OF PRIVATE PRAYER by John Baillie, copyright © 1949 by Charles Scribner's Sons and renewed 1977 by Ian Fowler Baillie (Simon & Schuster, 1996). Reprinted by kind permission of Scribner, Inc., and Oxford University Press; **273, 319, 320** from REVELATIONS OF DIVINE LOVE by Julian of Norwich, translated by Elizabeth Spearing, translation copyright © Elizabeth Spearing, 1998 (Penguin Classics). Reprinted by kind permission of the publishers; **293** from FROM DARKNESS TO LIGHT (POEMS AND PARABLES) by Jiddu Krishnamurti, copyright © Krishnamurti Foundation of America (Victor Gollancz, 1981); **299** from COLLECTED POEMS 1978–1998 by Craig Raine (Picador, 2000). Reprinted by kind permission of David Godwin Associates, London; **303** Reprinted by kind permission of Mrs Katrina Burnett, copyright © Mrs Katrina Burnett (The Estate of Eiluned Lewis); **307** from THE GREAT CHIEF SENDS WORD. Distributed by One Village, Chalbury, OX7 35Q; **335** from SELECTED POEMS by Yehuda Amichai (Faber & Faber, 2000). Reprinted by kind permission of the publishers; **337** from ANAM CARA: SPIRITUAL WISDOM FROM THE CELTIC FAITH by John

O'Donohue (Bantam Press). Reprinted by kind permission of Transworld Publishers, a division of the Random House Group Ltd, London; **338** from TESTAMENT OF YOUTH by Vera Brittain (Virago Press, 1992). Reprinted by kind permission of her literary executors, Mark Bostridge and Rebecca Williams, and Victor Gollancz Ltd; **347** from THE COLLECTED POEMS 1934–1953 by Dylan Thomas (Orion Paperbacks, 2000). Reprinted by kind permission of David Higham Associates, London, and New Directions Publishing Corporation, New York; **354** from COLLECTED POEMS by Theodore Roethke (Bantam Dell Publishing, 1978). Reprinted by kind permission of the publishers.

The publishers have made every effort to contact copyright holders. We should like to apologize for any errors or omissions, which we will endeavour to rectify in future printings of this book.

The publishers would like to thank Hanne Bewernick, Catherine Bradley and Tony Allan for their advice on the selection of quotations for this book.

photographic credits

The publisher would like to thank the following people, museums and photographic libraries for permission to reproduce their material. Every care has been taken to trace copyright holders. However, if we have omitted anyone we apologize and will, if informed, make corrections in future printings.

Page 2 digitalvision/Robert Harding Picture Library, London (ARC); **5** Photonica, London/H. Sakuramoto; **6** Photonica/Tatsuo Izuka; **8** Photonica/Jo Sugimura; **11** ImageState, London; **12–13** Corbis/Michael Yamashita; **14** Getty, London/Imagebank; **16** Photonica/Andrew Southon; **18** Getty/Imagebank; **20–21** Photonica/Michael Gersinger; **22** Getty/Stone; **25** Photonica/Yoshiki Komei; **26–27** Getty/Telegraph; **28** Photonica/Bruno Ehrs; **30** ARC; **32–33** Getty/Stone; **34–35** ARC; **36** Photonica/Johner; **38–39** Getty/Telegraph; **40–41** Photonica/Kazumi Nagasawa; **42** Photonica/Henry Horenstein; **44** Getty/Stone; **47** ImageState; **48–49** ARC; **50–51** ARC; **53** Getty/Telegraph; **56–57** Photonica/Carlos Saito; **58** Getty/Stone; **60** ARC; **62** Getty/Stone; **64** Photonica/David H. Wells; **66** Getty/Telegraph; **70** Getty/Stone; **75** Getty/Stone; **79** Getty/Food Pix; **82** Getty/Stone; **86–87** Getty/Imagebank; **88–89** Getty/Imagebank; **92** Photonica/Y. Takahashi; **94** Getty/Imagebank; **96** Photonica/Takeshmi Kanzaki; **98** Photonica/Johner; **103** Photonica/Teisuke Shinoda; **106** Photonica/Jean Claude Meighan; **108** Getty/Telegraph; **110–111** Photonica/Richard Boll; **113** Getty/Stone;

114 Getty/Imagebank; **117** Photonica/Karen Cipolla; **118** Photonica/Wilhem Scholz; **120–121** Getty/Imagebank; **122** Getty/Imagebank; **124** Getty/Imagebank; **126–127** Photonica/David Zaita; **130–131** Photonica/Johner; **132–133** Getty/Stone; **134–135** Getty/Stone; **136** Photonica/Minori Kawana; **138–139** Getty/Food Pix; **140–141** Getty/Stone; **144** Photonica/Bjorn Keller; **146–147** Getty/Stone; **149** Photonica/Michael Darter; **151** Photonica/Doug Plummer; **153** Photonica/Doug Plummer; **156** Photonica/Johner; **158–159** Photonica/Elke Hessler; **160** Getty/Stone; **162** Getty/Stone; **166** Photonica/Yukari Ochiai; **168–169** Getty/FPG; **170-171** ARC; **175** Getty/Stone; **177** Getty/Imagebank; **178** ARC; **181** Getty/Stone; **182–183** Getty/Stone; **184** ARC; **187** Getty/Imagebank; **188** Getty/Imagebank; **190–191** Getty/Imagebank; **192** Photonica/Jed Share; **195** Getty/FPG; **198** Photonica/Markus Naumann; **201** Getty/Stone; **203** Photonica/Yoshinori Watabe; **205** Photonica/Pascal Menard; **206** ARC; **208–209** Getty/Imagebank; **210** Photonica/Tadashi Ono; **212** Photonica/Keijro Komine; **215** Photonica/Tatsuo Izuka; **216** Getty/Stone; **218** Photonica/Akio Seo; **223** Photonica/Tadashi Ono; **224** Photonica/Syusuke Nakemura; **226** Getty/Imagebank; **229** Getty/Imagebank; **230** Getty/Stone; **234–235** Getty/Imagebank; **237** Getty/Stone; **238** Photonica/Tamarra Richards; **241** Photonica/Richard Seagrave; **242** Getty/Imagebank; **244** Getty/Telegraph